THE LANCASHIRE HEELER

SECOND BOOK

By

KATHIE KIDD – England

and

EEVA-MAIJA LEHTINEN – Finland, Scandinavia

Published by Kathleen B. Kidd
Newlands, 10 Parkway, Bognor Regis, Sussex PO21 2XR, England

ISBN 0-9543476-0-9

"The Lancashire Heeler" – Second Book

Printed by Bernard Kaymar Ltd,
Trout Street, Preston, Lancashire PR1 4DL Tel: 01772 562211 Fax: 01772 257813
E-mail: sales@bernard-kaymar.co.uk

DISCLAIMER

Careful research has been undertaken to supply details for this book. However, the authors disclaim responsibility for any inaccuracies as some subjects needed information supplied from other sources.

CONTENTS

ILLUSTRATIONS

PREFACE

Introduction to the second book of the Lancashire Heeler with update from 1990 (when the "First Book of the Lancashire Heeler incorporating the First Lancashire Heeler Handbook" was published). The first book sold out success-fully with many appreciated remarks about its usefulness. For the past few years many people have asked where a copy could be obtained, and the only copies available were second-hand. In fact requirement was there to such an extent that seemingly the First Edition has become a Collector's item with a price tag I never dreamed of.

Owing to demand I've been approached many times to produce another work on the Lancashire Heeler. So after a period of 11 years, here is the second book which updates many aspects, new subjects and revised text, many different various photos, also incorporating a Picture Gallery and Advertisement section. These could be useful for future owners and enthusiasts to check if or where any conformation changes may occur.

There are many stories told concerning the Lancashire Heeler and many things have happened, all of which is impossible to compress into a production of this size. So for reasons of page space, (like the dog), it has to be "Multum in Parvo" (much in little!).

It is now 24 years since the original Founder members formed the (unofficial) Lancashire Heeler Club in 1978. But it became Kennel Club Registered in 1983. During that time more people worldwide have become acquainted with the breed and now there are clubs in Sweden, Holland and Finland has a strong contingent as well as several other countries where numbers may be small, but dogs have been exported from the U.K. All the time interest is growing.

Since the breed obtained Pedigree status in 1981, the ensuing years have attracted many more followers. Many more breed classes have been scheduled at all Show levels including Championship Shows (where since 1999 Challenge Certificates have been allocated to some) thus with the advent of CCs now the title of Champion can be and has been attained in the U.K.

Formerly classified as a Rare Breed in the Working Group, this was changed in 1999 when the breed was transferred into the Pastoral Group. Also later that same year after discussion at the A.G.M. application was made to the Kennel Club to allow the colour of liver and tan (as well as black and tan) to be allowed in the Breed Standard, which the K.C. permitted.

In 1996 a Meeting took place to form another Breed Club in the U.K. to be known as the East of England (proposed) Lancashire Heeler Club. This is unofficial as at the time of writing no application has been made to register it, but due to circum-stances some people from East Anglia felt the need for another club. It has proved very popular with organised events and financially successful. No doubt in the fullness of time there may well be other regional clubs where a need is felt, as has happened with most other longer established breeds.

References are made in the book to Mrs Gwen Mackintosh, the lady whose enthusiasm inspired others which collectively led to eventually resulting in the Lancashire Heeler Club. It had never been Gwen's intention to pioneer the breed as it all started purely as a personal hobby for the love of the dogs, but when events led to it becoming a Pedigree dog, it has taken its place alongside other longer, established breeds. (Refer to chapter on history "A Pedigree Dog 1981"). She did so much for the breed and was the first Lancashire Heeler Club President. (I knew her personally and worked with her when serving on the Lancashire Heeler Club Committee for about 10 years during which time I held various positions retiring as Chairman in 1992). Gwen always had the well-being of the dogs at heart; she was not a commercial breeder. In fact, I think to start with, when any puppies were born, she gave them away to friends she knew who would provide good homes. Latterly she sold to selected people, but she never charged much (not even what was then the "going" rate). Her dogs slept in the house on little beds. I remember this well as the beds had white sheets on! I asked why, and this was if any bitch showed signs of coming into season, immediately Gwen would know, so that she could keep the bitch away from any dogs, because Gwen never abused her bitches with too much breeding, so tried to avoid accidental matings. Although living in Norfolk (because of the family business of Mackintosh's Sweets, "Quality Street" and many other products where the family had a factory as well as in Halifax) Gwen came from Yorkshire and had a very practical outlook with a lovely sense of humour. She could be a great raconteur as her life had been eventful with the business connections and dogs (she had another affix for her Boxers of Macbrook, (made up of half of Mackintosh and half of the village of Brooke), where their magnificent almost stately home had been built by her husband. There were extensive grounds as Gwen also had a Pedigree herd of cows as a hobby. Also in the grounds were staff houses. When Gwen's husband died, the big house was sold and she had a beautiful new one built which was named "Acremead" (the affix she used for her Heelers). With the new house she kept 100 acres for her dogs to run on!

We visited and stayed with Gwen and sometimes we would look at old photos seeing some of her former dogs and some earlier days of social connections with Society which had included royalty. Then later on when Gwen was Life Vice President of the Norfolk & Norwich Canine Society, I think she accompanied the present Queen around when she was on a visit to the show.

Often some of the early Committee Meetings were held at "Acremead" and afterwards there would be much laughing when Gwen started talking. Also some early Committee Meetings were held at the home of a Founder Member Mrs Dolly Rush, who had an inglenook fireplace where burning logs gave out a welcome heat. After those Committee Meetings could also be jolly when Dolly would be asked to play her electric organ in the lounge, as we indulged in her lovely homemade cakes! (Was it surprising most Committee Members attended when entertainment afterwards was so pleasurable?) These recollections of the Club's early days have many happy memories.

Sadly in July 1992, Gwen died and her passing was a great loss to the breed and to the Club.

In December 1992, sadly for me, Mrs Barbara Kidd, my mother died who had always been very supportive in all things I had done regarding dogs over many years. As catering was our business, many times my mother organised the food for events; both for the Lancashire Heeler Club, also when I was Chairman of the South East Corgi Association. There were many lunches and dinners given. Before her passing, our dog interests were in partnership in every sense of the word, to me she was a pillar of integrity. Over the years we travelled thousands of miles to Dog Shows, Committee Meetings, Dog Events etc.

Then in 2001 another stalwart for Lancashire Heelers, Mr Ellis Garner, mentioned in the book, died. His knowledge of them was tremendously useful as his family could trace back having kept them for well over 160 years. My mother and I sometimes visited him and his wife Betty and I met his mother Mrs Grace Garner (who has since died) who told me about when she was a little girl and growing up with Heelers.

Ellis had been very helpful even before the Breed or Club was recognised as his co-operation was greatly appreciated by Founder Members. Ellis lived in Hoscar, Lancashire, near Ormskirk, the area which is often associated with early reports of the breed (refer to chapter "History of the Lancashire Heeler"). Ellis will be greatly missed.

Over the years the exposure through showing has increased the interest in the breed by both genuine pet lovers and the dog showing fraternity. It is sincerely hoped that anyone, anywhere, being an owner of this small intelligent breed will endeavour to maintain its characteristics as the current Standard requires and that through the passage of time fashionable trends sometimes resulting through showing will not spoil its size, temperament, agility or many other capabilities, all of which add to its unusual charm.

It is hoped that the breed will not be exploited by profiteers. The Lancashire Heeler Club has a Code of Ethics incorporated with Club Rules for its members, setting out guidelines that bitches should not be abused with too much puppy production. Already in the U.K. many breeds of unfortunate dogs have been found straying or ill treated and put into dog homes. Responsible, caring Lancashire Heeler enthusiasts would not want to add to that list of forsaken dogs.

Maybe a few critics will find something unfavourable in these writings, but everything is meant with the best of good intentions to help to preserve the well-being and characteristics of this very small dog (as we know it now!)

The information in this book covers many aspects including the life expectancy of a Lancashire Heeler which can be long, so anyone thinking of buying one should not do so flippantly, as a dog is a faithful companion, and with luck a Lancashire Heeler could be with you and your household for at least 10 years or more.

Many owners love them and would not be without one, finding them to have so much character often found in larger dogs, and yet they are so very small, very active, clean, good guard dogs with affectionate temperaments to have in the house.

An unusual feature of some Lancashire Heelers is their "smile". When pleased some draw back their lips, showing their closed teeth and usually wagging their tails and wriggling to show their great pleasure.

Personally, whilst liking all dogs, and having kept several breeds over the years, our family choice has been Pembroke Welsh Corgis, followed by Lancashire Heelers. Keeping both Corgis and Lancashire Heelers it has been interesting to observe there are several similar characteristics in both breeds, not least the "heeling" instinct. Lancashire Heelers are quicker and faster (because of their size, notably daylight under the body and lighter build) than a Corgi. Our dogs have always lived in the house as part of our family and whilst dearly loving our Corgis, it is noticeable that the different sleek, short smooth coat of the Lancashire Heeler with less profuse density does not shed anything like the amount of hairs as Corgis do, thus the Lancashire Heeler coat means less vacuum cleaning or carpet brushing!

Different breeds suit different people. This book has set out to attempt to give a general idea of the smallest English (Yes, surely it can claim this unless future evidence might prove otherwise) Pastoral dog. For generations past in the North of England it has given useful work and pleasure to those who kept it. No doubt in the future many more people will come to know and wish to own a Lancashire Heeler and experience the delight this little dog can be.

Kathleen B. (Kathie) Kidd, 2002

ACKNOWLEDGEMENTS

In compiling this book it has been my intention to include as much information as possible relating to the Lancashire Heeler. I would like to thank the following people for their response and co-operation for contributions:-

First, to Miss Eeva Maija Lehtinen for great assistance with photographs, drawings and articles on Lancashire Heelers in Finland and Sweden. Her help has been most useful. For many years she has enthusiastically followed the progress of the breed, consequently flying many, many times to England furthering her knowledge and updating her records.

Eeva was no stranger to dogs already having bred and kept Champion Dachshunds and Corgis before owning and breeding Champion Lancashire Heelers. She is an experienced judge and much respected in Finland for her canine work. Eeva is an Honorary Member of the Finnish Welsh Corgi Club and was awarded the honour of "Suamen Kennelliiton Hopeinen Ansiomerkki" (From the Finnish Kennel Club).

To all those people who have kindly sent in photographs of their Lancashire Heelers. This collection, showing some of today's types will prove a useful reference for the future. Everywhere, where known, those who submitted photos have sought permission and credits are mentioned.

To Miss Jackie Reid for her most descriptive article on Training in Obedience, Agility and Working Trials which is accompanied with some excellent action photos (credits given).

To Miss Jacky Cutler for her contribution concerning Eyes and update explanations of problems.

To Mrs Wendy Lewis (a former Lancashire Heeler Club Secretary) for her detailed and highly useful lengthy article (based on her experience) of breeding Lancashire Heeler puppies. Entitled "Don't Panic", it is so descriptive and many favourable comments about it from readers of "The First Book of the Lancashire Heeler" warrant it to be included again, and Wendy has revised and updated anything she considered necessary.

To Mrs Betty Garner for permission to reproduce old photographs showing the late Mr Ellis Garner as a boy with the family's Lancashire Heelers. His late mother, Mrs Grace Garner appears on these photos.

The "Evening News" (Norwich) for permission to reproduce the original photo taken in 1978 when the first Breed Standard for Lancashire Heelers was formulated.

To the Kennel Club (London) for permission to use the current Breed Standard (as at 1999).

Thanks to Dick Koster for his contribution from Holland on "The Lancashire Heeler in the Netherlands".

SOME LANCASHIRE HEELERS SHOWING VARYING TYPES WITH DIFFERENT EARS AND TAIL CARRIAGE POSITIONS
(All acceptable)

Photo by: E.M. LEHTINEN

Pictured:

Top left: **CH. KALO SUPER SHADOW** (Finland from England)

Top Right: **KALO BIRTHDAY PRINCE** (Finland from England)

Centre left: **BOWANNE LOLLYPOP LIL** (Finland from England)

Centre: **CH. STARDOGS VA'DU'VILL** (Finland from Sweden)

Centre right: **CH. EIJATUUN WELLCOME SANTA** (Finland)

Bottom: **LANKEELA FLY BY NIGHT TO KALO** (England)

USES OF THE LANCASHIRE HEELER
AS A WORKING DOG
(In the Pastoral Group since 1999)

This small breed is amazing for its versatility. Essentially it is a "Heeling Dog" (as the name implies). Therefore it was (and still is in places) used in the same manner as a Corgi, to drive cattle by "nipping" at the cows "heels", which was a great help to farmers. Also in bygone days when cattle would be driven to abattoirs, these small dogs would be sometimes known as "Butchers dogs", as they barked or snapped behind the cows, driving them along. Cattle heeling and sheep are perhaps their most quoted attributes, but some have a knack of rounding up other animals too, including chickens.

WORKING CATTLE AND SHEEP

Despite many nowadays being kept as pets some can still do the same job as their ancestors. One Lancashire Heeler in particular should be mentioned. This is Pepi of Winder, a bitch belonging to Mr and Mrs Morphet of Cumbria. Every day Pepi works and if required will position herself at an open gate of a field of cows, and hold the cows in alone. She does this by barking or snapping at cows, should they try to wander out. This is particularly useful when the tractor has to be taken into the field (with a load of hay etc). It means the tractor driver is saved having to dismount twice! He gets off to open the gate, and drives through. Then Pepi takes over guarding the entrance. After work has been done in the field, the driver drives out, then dismounts to close the gate for the final time. However long it takes in the field, Pepi makes sure no cows escape! Also she drives sheep up to the fells when wanted. Sometimes the sheep are reluctant to go, but Pepi urges them on. Pepi has a daughter Chainy's Gem, and she too is following in Mother's footsteps. Mrs Morphet also shows, and Pepi has won many prizes in her role as a Pedigree dog. Sometimes she has been out working the cattle in mud just a mere 6 hours before appearing at a Dog Show and arrived looking clean and nicely presented and has won her class easily. This illustrates that a working dog can be a successful Show Dog, and vice versa. Sadly, since this was written, Pepi has died. Others are used on farms in Sweden and England, notably Mr & Mrs Patrick's Lancashire Heelers who work sheep and round up for market.

VERSATILITY

Another highly useful attribute of many Lancashire Heelers is their ability to catch vermin. Farmers who have always had rats or mice problems, found their Lancashire Heelers soon made short work of them. So many were kept as vermin hunters around the farm buildings.

SOME USES OF THE LANCASHIRE HEELER

*Herding Sheep – Joan & John Patrick's RUPERT (Patterjo Shoeshine Boy)
helps a lot on the farm.*

Photo by: J. PATRICK

*DANIEL (Sandpits Wild Garlic) and ELLIS (Sandpits Monkshood)
Working cows in Sweden, August 1991.*

Photo by: K.B. KIDD

The Lancashire Heeler has a good reputation as a rabbiting dog, being able to flush them out easily. (It has been said that some Lancashire Heelers might have been favoured by poachers, as their handy size was small enough to hide in an inside pocket of the old style raincoat! For this, the smaller the size of the dog was the better!)

Also some Lancashire Heelers were, and still are, used as Shooting Dogs. Mr Ellis Garner has used his for shooting.

It is known too, that Lancashire Heelers were kept for ferreting.

Some are known to like water, and will catch fish in shallow water. (Not all like water). Some whose walks take them on beaches or along estuaries have a keen nose for finding various living things under stones or around rocks etc.

Another use is that of bird scarer! Where birds prove a menace to fish stocked ponds or streams, if asked Lancashire Heelers will soon adapt to chasing off the birds.

Some Lancashire Heelers are used as companions for race horses, and go with horses when travelling in horse boxes, to help "settle" the horses. Lancashire Heelers and horses usually get along well.

A popular use is an excellent guard dog around the home, protecting its property. It is quickly roused, and raises the alarm when strangers are about.

As agreeable companions most Lancashire Heelers are excellent. Most are known to be very affectionate and faithful to their owners.

INTELLIGENCE

Some have very good directional sense, and are said to be able to "point". One is known to show its farmer owner where a hare is to be found by "pointing".

Some with their amazing intelligence have proved to be life-savers! There was the case of a Dachshund who on the scent of the rabbit, got itself stuck in a warren in a sand quarry, and was both far in and deep down. The human ear could not hear any sound at all. The Dachshund's owner, Mrs Wendy Lewis, also had her Lancashire Heeler "Eccles" (Stonebridge Ashley of Sandpits) with her whilst searching for the lost Dachshund. Eccles got to a certain point and would not move. He "told" where the lost dog was, which was a place not suspected. Since Eccles gave this signal, both Wendy and her husband Mr Mike Lewis dug furiously down until it was evident that they were at the right spot. Wendy put herself in danger and crawled to retrieve the Dachshund safely. But without the accurate sense of location of Eccles, the story may well not have had a happy ending.

Another Lancashire Heeler woke his sleeping owners by barking during the night and this probably saved their lives, as a fire had broken out in part of the house. The Lancashire Heeler smelling the smoke enabled all to evacuate safely and get the Fire Service before too much damage resulted.

SOME USES OF THE LANCASHIRE HEELER

FLY (Lankeela Fly By Night to Kalo) retrieving a pigeon.

Owned and Photographed by: K.B. KIDD

SANDPITS SAFFRON with a killed rat.

Owned and photographed by: WENDY LEWIS

11

SOME USES OF THE LANCASHIRE HEELER

POPPETT (Patterjo Gingham) with pig, "Oink"

Owned and Photographed by: JOAN PATRICK

Lancashire Heeler sharing fireside with goat, belonging to Elaine & Ken Moore

THERAPEUTIC

It is known that some dogs in general, can be therapeutic. Lancashire Heelers are no exception. Mr James Pack, of Sussex, was suffering from high blood pressure and not in good health. Then he thought a little dog (a Lancashire Heeler) might be a nice idea for him, to help cheer him up. Mr Pack had seen and loved Mrs W. Lewis's little "Spinner", and as the dog liked him so much, Mrs Lewis let Mr Pack have her, and so it was not long before he and Spinner began going for short walks, which soon became longer walks! His health improved greatly. After a while the Doctor was very pleased to report that the blood pressure had improved dramatically. Mr Pack attributed his better health to the endearing qualities and interest inspired by Spinner.

This is not the only case where a Lancashire Heeler and the interest it has brought has helped to improve the health of a human. Another true report came from Cumbria, where Mrs Elaine Moore knew of Mr Austin who had retired, had a heart attack and felt that life was rather dull. This worried his wife who thought a Lancashire Heeler might cheer him up. So Mrs Moore was contacted and able to supply a little Lancashire Heeler called "Scamp". After having Scamp, Mr Austin felt a new man and found after a short while he was able to go long walks, sometimes as far as four miles. (It has been realised by many that not only Lancashire Heelers, but some other dogs too, prove very helpful with some people if they have been in poor health). Several are used as "PAT" dogs visiting people in hospital where they proved popular.

Another, perhaps unusual use, was where a Lancashire Heeler used to help collect the eggs with her owner. This was Classic Crown owned by Mrs Enid Lord, who kept chickens and when egg collecting Classic Crown (a bitch) used to pick up the eggs in her mouth and take them to Mrs Lord, who really found this very helpful.

In Finland, owner Mrs Anja Hietamies was very pleased with her Lancashire Heeler Riku (Kalo Birthday Prince) and his guarding abilities. Late one night she was driving along with Riku in torrential rain, until the weather became so bad she decided to stop in a layby, and sleep for a few hours. Suddenly she awoke to see Riku snarling and barking furiously out at the dark. Flashing a light she saw three youths creeping towards the car menacingly. But the more the dog barked, so they slowed, and eventually turned away. They could not see, only hear the Lancashire Heeler which Mrs Hietamies feels sure, prevented her from being robbed or attacked in her car.

THE FIRST LANCASHIRE HEELER TO GAIN C.D.EX. TITLE

As well as all of the useful working ways, some Lancashire Heelers are found to be very good at Obedience, Agility and Field Trials. The first one to receive the title of C.D.Ex. U.D.Ex is "Dinah" (Sandpits Wood Sage) belonging to Miss Jackie Reid, and bred by Mrs Wendy Lewis. Miss Reid had had considerable experience with other dogs but Dinah was her first Lancashire Heeler to train and she found Dinah learned in half the time of some others. (A fuller article appears in this book on the subject, by Jackie).

(C.D. Ex. = Companion Dog Excellent) (U.D. Ex = Utility Dog Excellent)

REFER TO CHAPTER "TRAINING THE LANCASHIRE HEELER IN OBEDIENCE, AGILITY AND WORKING TRIALS".

LANCASHIRE HEELERS USED AS THERAPEUTIC

Photo shows RISEHILL JUST WILLIAM CD.Ex., UD.Ex, (Bill)
ready in uniform as a "PETS AS THERAPY DOG". Dog owned by Jackie Reid.

Photo by: B. GUARD

SOME USES OF THE LANCASHIRE HEELER

*LAUSTEPH CLANCIE TRAQDEAN (Baachus) and
HAELARBOBS ULURU AT TRAQDEAN (Emma) with caught rabbit.*

Owned and photographed by: TRACY ST. CLAIR PEARCE

Drawing by Eeva Lehtinen of Acremead Biscuit of Kalo

TRAINING THE LANCASHIRE HEELER IN OBEDIENCE, AGILITY AND WORKING TRIALS

By Jackie Reid

CHOICE OF DOG

The choice of dog is very important if you wish to train your dog for Kennel Club Working Competitions. Try and get a good breed specimen as your dog will meet many more people and become better known to a much larger audience than any of the non-working Breed Champions!

1. TEMPERAMENT

The puppy has to be well socialised with the breeder and with you and has to be good with people and to tolerate and be controlled with other dogs. Any dog that attempts to bite people is not suitable. Very important the dog is not sound sensitive and is not frightened of loud noises. Sound sensitiveness may be hereditary so it is important that you do not buy a puppy from a very frightened timid bitch.

2. PHYSIQUE AND HEALTH

It is easier to train slightly larger dogs than smaller ones and a truly working heeler may rest but is never tired. Only ever buy from eye tested stock so you know the status of your dogs eyes. Mild CEA provided you do not wish to breed is no bar to a working dog. Check with the breeder about the prevalence of lens luxation but unfortunately it is impossible to tell if the dog is affected until it happens.

TRAINING

Start your dog on Obedience Training when it is still a puppy and if you use one of the modern methods such as 'clicker' training linked with firmness I have found even the most headstrong Heeler will respond. If you wish to show your dog in the breed ring there is no reason why you cannot do both at the same time.

OBEDIENCE COMPETITIONS

The Obedience exercises for the early Obedience Competitions are as follows: Heelwork off and on the lead, recall, retrieve and the stays. All these exercises are suitable for Heelers but it is very important to go to a class that understands all breeds and uses motivational methods. If your dog is bored with Obedience it is usually the case that incorrect methods have been used.

TRAINING THE LANCASHIRE HEELER IN OBEDIENCE, AGILITY AND WORKING TRIALS

SANDPITS WOODSAGE CD.Ex, UD.Ex, (Dinah) seen at Working Trials long jump

Photo by permission of MARGOT OSBORNE

SANDPITS WOODSAGE CD.Ex, UD.Ex, (Dinah) seen at Working Trials clear jump.
Owned by Jackie Reid.

Photo by: C. GUARD

AGILITY

The Lancashire Heeler is less than 15" in height so it is in the category of Mini dog and jumps are 15". Most Heelers have no difficulty with jumping and the apparatus and enjoy agility. It is important to learn control and it helps to go to Obedience Classes first. Both dog and handler have to be as fit as possible and age for the handler need not be a problem as I know people with disabilities and in their eighties competing.

It is a good idea to practice indoors in riding schools as well as outside as a dog may decide to go off for a hunt if they are not used to being outside! The age dogs are allowed to compete is 18 months old.

About 15 dogs have over the years competed or are competing in agility.

WORKING TRIALS

Working Trials is a combination of Agility, Obedience and Nosework. Small dogs are only able to compete in the 2 lower stakes, which are Companion Dog and Utility Dog, in the other stakes the jumps are not lowered. It is very important and much easier if the dog is tough and does not mind the mud and the rain and heavy cover. Some of the conditions in Working Trials may be very rough and a country dog from a farm background is preferable. If you have a sound sensitive dog, you have to overcome this problem as one of the exercises is steadiness to gunshot.

1. CONTROL (OBEDIENCE) SECTION

   In this section the Obedience is very similar to the Obedience for Obedience Tests but not so accurate and is executed in a more natural manner. The exercises are heelwork recall, retrieving a dumb-bell and are able to do a sendaway of at least 100 yards. All the stays are out of sight and the other exercise is steadiness to gunshot. Extra commands are penalised.

2. AGILITY SECTION

   All the exercises in this section have to be done in a controlled manner and Heelers are represented in two heights of jumps. I have qualified a dog in each height range.

   Height of dog:

   Under 10"   Scale 3ft, clear jump 18", long jump 4ft

   Between 10" and 15"   Scale 4ft, clear jump 24", long jump 6ft

TRAINING THE LANCASHIRE HEELER IN OBEDIENCE, AGILITY AND WORKING TRIALS

SANDPITS HEMLOCK (Pepper, aged 10). Agility, Jumping.
Owned by Georgina Stout   Photo by: GEORGINA STOUT

SANDPITS TAGLIATELLE (Tag, aged 12) Agility Weaving Poles.
Owned by Georgina Stout   Photo by: GEORGINA STOUT

3. NOSEWORK SECTION

In the Companion Dog Stake the nosework consists of retrieving a dumb-bell and a simple search in a marked area.

In Utility Dog Stake this consists of a search and a track, which is half a mile long and half an hour old.

Heelers are very good trackers and mine are completely motivated by food and track in practice for their dinners. If you have a dog that likes hunting for rabbits you will probably be able to train it to track for human scent.

I know of three dogs that have competed in Working Trials, two of them qualified.

❖ ❖ ❖

(Drawing:E.M Lehtinen).

TRAINING THE LANCASHIRE HEELER IN OBEDIENCE, AGILITY AND WORKING TRIALS

Working Trials Scale

RISEHILL JUST WILLIAM
(Bill)
CD.Ex., UD.Ex.
Owned by Jackie Reid

Photo by C. GUARD

Agility Rigid Tunnel

DODDSLINE HAROLD
(Harry)
Owned by Lisa Hughes

Photo by L. HUGHES

ROLL OF HONOUR

These are the names of dogs that I know have done well in Open or Championship Competitions.

Agility

SENIOR DOGS

Jackie Reid's SANDPITS WOODSAGE CD.Ex., UD.Ex (Dinah)
First Heeler to compete in Open Agility.

Toni Sayer's LANKEELER LOCAL HERO (Foggy)

Novice Dogs with places and clear rounds

Jackie Reid's RISEHILL JUST WILLIAM CD.Ex., UD.Ex (Bill)

Jackie Reid's and Norman Johnston's DODDSLINE SPARKEY (Sparkey)

Toni Sayer's LANKEELER BECCA THE WRECKER (Becky)

Starter Dogs out of Elementary

Georgina Stout's SANDPITS HEMLOCK (Pepper)
Georgina Stout's SANDPITS TAGLIATELLE (Tag)

Working Trials

Jackie Reid's SANDPITS WOODSAGE CD.Ex., UD.Ex (Dinah)
The first Lancashire Heeler of either sex to qualify in Working Trials.

Jackie Reid's RISEHILL JUST WILLIAM CD.Ex., UD.Ex. (Bill)
The first Lancashire Heeler dog to qualify in Working Trials.

KC Good Citizen Awards

A number of Lancashire Heelers have been awarded
Bronze, Silver and Gold Awards.

The names of the Gold Awards are as follows:

Tony Hancock with RUDI

Jackie Reid with BILL and Jackie Reid with SPARKEY

DETAILS OF MY OWN DOGS
by Jackie Reid

Dinah was fairly easy to train but did not like heavy cover and had to be coaxed through difficulties. Had a thin coat and is quite touch sensitive and tolerates people. She was a very good jumper and would fling herself at anything. She is still alive at 16 years old. She is $9^{1}/_{2}$ inches high.

Bill came from Cumbria, grandmother worked on the fells (this is why I chose him). He has a thick heavy coat, which is ideal for going through brambles and other heavy cover. He is thick set and surprisingly is a very good jumper. Tracks and searches well but is not always committed to his task. Does a long galloping sendaway, which he must have inherited from collie ancestors. Very friendly with people and is a P.A.T. dog. He is $11^{3}/_{4}$ inches high.

Sparkey's ancestors worked cattle and he has very strong herding tendencies, which can be used in agility. Loves Obedience and I will compete with him in the spring. His agility has improved but I have had a long argument with him in the weaving poles, which I am winning! His Working Trial training has been held up with the Foot and Mouth epidemic. He tracks and at last has started to retrieve well. Sparkey is a very difficult dog to train because unless he finds his exercises exciting he goes to explore better things. I have had to make all training fully rewarding. Very friendly with people and is a P.A.T. dog. He is $11^{1}/_{2}$ inches high.

THE TEMPERAMENT OF LANCASHIRE HEELERS
(Questions often asked)

These questions are asked many times (and sensibly too).

What is the Temperament of a Lancashire Heeler like?

1.   Are they friendly?
2.   Do they get on with other dogs?
3.   Do they like children?
4.   Do they yap a lot?
5.   Are they suitable for elderly people?

1.   ARE THEY FRIENDLY?

Yes, Lancashire Heelers are mostly friendly. Most have the reputation of being happy dogs, as it takes very little cause for them to wag their tails with apparent pleasure. Also something which is peculiar to them is the **Lancashire Heeler "Smile"**. Many Lancashire Heelers when greeting their loved owners or friends will show their pleasure by decidedly "smiling" or laughing. This is raising the upper lips to reveal the teeth, usually accompanied by body wriggling.

But they will protect their territory and family or owners. So on first meeting the Lancashire Heeler (in common with other breeds) can be expected to be wary of strangers and some will keep their distance or show their reluctance to admit a stranger in, often raising their hackles and barking. But usually once they realise the stranger is acceptable to owners, most Lancashire Heelers will then run to, or jump up, and proceed to lick or kiss the visitor!

2.   DO THEY GET ON WITH OTHER DOGS?

Yes, often very well. In many cases people with Lancashire Heelers keep other breeds, and they agree. (But it has to be fairly mentioned, not in all cases). Many are known to co-exist most happily, but it does depend on the individual dogs concerned both ways, (which surely applies to many other breeds too). Some Lancashire Heelers can be very dominant and want to "boss", even among themselves. Several Lancashire Heelers owners who have experienced the "pack instinct" consider that Lancashire Heelers behave better kept in small numbers, and do not consider that they make good "pack dogs" as quarrels have resulted with sad consequences, on a few rare occasions. (It may be the case that some strains are either highly strung or more aggressive than others, which can be said of other breeds also). But in general the majority of Lancashire Heelers do live happily with another breed, and it is often the case that they will snuggle up to and go to sleep alongside another breed belonging to the same household.

3. DO THEY LIKE CHILDREN?

Yes, usually. But to be fair to these small dogs, they should not be bought as a plaything for a toy for children. Just because Lancashire Heelers are small, it would be unkind to buy one to be picked up, snatched up, or clawed at by uncontrolled and boisterous children, who might also have no compunction about dropping the dog. Because of its small size, little children could think it was eternally a puppy and be over zealous to pick it up. Children very often want to pick up small dogs by their front legs. This is very wrong and dangerous to the dog, because the entire weight of the dog is taken by the front legs. The bone structure of the dog is such that this places too much strain on the shoulders, which could suffer serious injury, also being painful.

Children should be taught to pick up the Lancashire Heeler (if they really need to) by supporting its weight by first placing their hand around the dog's body (the rib cage) and then immediately by supporting the dog's bottom (rump) with their other hand and then carefully lifting the dog and tucking it close to their own body, so that it has firm support and comfort. (But it is up to parents to ensure that children are kind and respect the feelings of the dog. Remembering that children can speak but dogs can't).

Most Lancashire Heelers like or love children who treat them kindly. Most Lancashire Heelers will enjoy playing games, especially balls, which they like to retrieve. There are many instances where Lancashire Heelers and children are devoted to each other, which is a joy to see. Where children and dogs are concerned there should be a heavy commitment to educate both to respect the other. For safety reasons the parents should discourage their children from putting their faces or hands near to unknown dogs (of any breed).

4. DO THEY YAP A LOT?

Because it is small, some people think that Lancashire Heelers might be yappers. The answer is not in general. Most Lancashire Heelers have good quality guarding instincts and will bark to protect their surroundings (be it house, garden or car etc.). But most have a reasonably deepish sounding "doggy bark". As with most breeds, how much and how often they bark, sometimes is a reflection of its environment or training, or whether from a more highly strung strain, which is general to most dogs. Properly trained, most Lancashire Heelers are not "yappers".

5. ARE THEY SUITABLE FOR ELDERLY PEOPLE?

In many ways, yes, but Lancashire Heelers are quick to move about. As a house dog they are highly suited for elderly people in that they are so clean about the house, not having a long hairy coat to drop and make work to clean up. Also they are easily to pick up. They are (as has already been mentioned) excellent guard dogs, to give warning of strangers approaching. They are affectionate, and like being fussed by sitting on knees etc. They enjoy walking. Although small, the Lancashire Heeler needs exercise, they do not like being shut up without having a garden to run in, or regular walks. A lot is to be said in their favour for elderly people, apart from the fact that the Lancashire Heeler can move so fast, in some cases they might prove too quick where an elderly person might be incapacitated themselves, and not able to grab hold of the dog quick enough if, for example, the door should be opened, the dog could run out through it's owner's legs, in a trice! Whereas with a bigger dog, there would be more to clutch at to stop it escaping! Also when travelling in cars, where a person might be slow at getting in or out, they would have to ensure that the Lancashire Heeler did not jump out, as they can move in a flash through such a small space, where a bigger dog could not get through.

But many elderly people do have Lancashire Heelers and adore them, saying they are marvellous for them, as they have so much dog character in such a small body around their house, and they are so easy to care for. As in so many cases, it all depends on the situation for each owner and the dog concerned.

(Where elderly owners might encounter a problem with car travelling with their Lancashire Heelers, they could always have a dog travelling cage on the back seat, and putting the Lancashire Heeler in this would ensure safety, about not jumping out. Or of course the passenger could always keep hold of the lead securely).

GROOMING

Because of its short, sleek coat, and mostly black or liver colour coat, the Lancashire Heeler is very easy to care for. But it likes to be brushed, with a fairly soft brush. Also the coat can be made shinier by grooming with a piece of velvet or silk cloth, or this is often achieved with lots of daily stroking.

BATHING

A Lancashire Heeler is easy, although they don't need it as often as many other breeds.

DEWCLAWS AND NAILS

Where dewclaws have been left on they should be checked to see that a complete circle is nor forming, which might become a potential hazard. If so, they should be trimmed as should other nails if they get too long. (Mostly Lancashire Heeler's nails keep suitably worn naturally.

I'M A HEELER

I'm a Lancashire Heeler, What's that you may say?
So just stop and listen, please don't go away.
My ancestors come from the Lancashire Dales,
With pricked ears and bright eyes, and proudly held tails.
I'm small, dark and handsome, with a shiny black coat,
And touches of dark brown at ears, feet and throat.
No, I'm not a lap dog – if that's what you thought,
In fact I am perfectly fashioned for sport,
With strong stocky front and powerful paws,
For rat holes and rabbits and all things outdoors.
I'm bright and alert and I don't miss a thing.
The rustle of fur, or the brush of a wing,
There's many a rabbit or pheasant would cry,
The day that a Lancashire Heeler came by.
From pedigree background, though still rather rare,
My impeccable breeding gives much to compare,
With other small breeds, at Cruft's you will see,
Because I'm a Lancashire Heeler ... That's me!

EARL BUMBLE BEE!

By Mrs Sheila Curson of Rackheath, Norwich

Editors Note: This was written before colour liver & tan was permitted in the breed standard

HISTORY OF THE LANCASHIRE HEELER
(From "The First Book of the Lancashire Heeler")

Reliable, recorded, documented history of the Lancashire Heeler seems hard to find. Therefore, what is known can only be relatively brief. Most is by word of mouth, and so could be subject to speculation. A number of channels have been explored including several libraries which have been visited in Lancashire, which have produced very little result. In fact, to date, nothing found there was not already known. Ormskirk Library, itself (the area from where the Lancashire Heeler is reputed to have had earliest Lancashire known origins) had such scant information when enquiries were made in 1983, that the Librarian at the time was pleased to learn of any more Lancashire Heeler information that could be sent to them, since they often had inquiries on the breed, and were unaware at the time that even a Lancashire Heeler Club existed which could be referred to.

Since most history has been by word of mouth, some has been worth recording, but a considerable amount is better discarded, as time has proved quite a lot to be imaginative conjecture.

Some short references to the Lancashire Heeler are contained in a few old books. One reference goes back to 1486 (but whether this was in fact a Lancashire Heeler, or a dog resembling it, is a matter of opinion. It should be remembered a number of old drawings show "turn spit" dogs, and simply because they might have been small and black does not mean they were Lancashire Heelers). (I possess a photo taken of an old etching which shows what appears to be a Lancashire Heeler accompanying Horsemen at "The Meet". Despite research, its origin is still uncertain).

THE NAME

The name Lancashire Heeler has been used by many Lancastrians for as long as they can remember. One who authenticates this is Mr Ellis Garner, whose family can easily trace having consistently kept the breed for at least 160 years. His mother, Mrs Grace Garner, has old photos which shows her as a little girl with her Grandmother holding Lancashire Heelers in their arms. She remembers her grandparents always kept them on their farms. Mr Ellis Garner lived near Ormskirk, as has his family before him, and they always referred to the breed as Lancashire Heelers.

However, there are references too, to the name of Ormskirk Heeler. This is found in the "Dog Owner's Encyclopaedia", by Brian Vesey-Fitzgerald. A short quote says, "Ormskirk Heeler. A corgi type dog, a typical Heeler, not uncommon in the North of England and increasing in popularity. Not recognised by the Kennel Club. Colour; usually Black and Tan. Height about 13 inches". Also word of mouth has had a few references to the Name of Ormskirk Terrier. It would seem that as the breed was unrecognised (by the Kennel Club) for so long, that the name of the breed was a matter of local choice.

When the K.C. recognised the breed in 1981, the official name of Lancashire Heeler was registered. This appears the most logical as it embraced the county and not all had been confined to Ormskirk. Others had been in various parts of Lancashire and surrounding areas. Also by 1981, a considerable number were in the county of Norfolk too.

THEORIES OF ORIGIN

Theories as to the history abound but, as yet, are not born out by authentic proof. Among them are that the Lancashire Heeler goes back to Saxon times. Later, there have been a number of reports of a titled Gentleman (was it a Lord?) having established a large kennel of Lancashire Heelers, and he had tried to breed them with great care, so that it is said he had fixed a good type. But it is thought this kennel was disbanded at the outbreak of a war (which one remains uncertain), as the owner left England and went abroad. It is thought that then some of these dogs went to some people who when they bred continued to try to keep the breed pure. But that other people who had them did not worry, so let cross matings happen by accident or lack of interest for the breed. It is also thought whoever the Lord (?) was, had tried to get the breed recognised. Where he began is again lost in the past. But another theory is that someone had gone to Germany and brought back a very small black and tan dog, like a Lancashire Heeler. But it could not have been the same man, as the timing would not have fitted. We must also bear in mind that Mr Garner's family had them for going back at least 160 years, which would be long before the First World War. So this breed must have been long established in Lancashire, even assuming if it had been introduced from another country. That theory has produced so many different countries that a selection includes Germany, France, Ireland, Belgium, Australia, China and Wales! It seems that from each of these countries someone has likened another similar dog to the Lancashire Heeler.

But with all the varying theories we are still waiting for 100% proof that any single one may be the authentic origin. Therefore, at this stage, it seems better to keep an open mind about the Lancashire Heelers earliest known history. But for good measure a few more references include the following, which are at a later period.

A newspaper article in "OUR DOGS", published December, 21, 1956, written by Macdonald Daly says, "My attention was first drawn to "Heelers" during one of my judging visits to Lancashire, when Mr Robert Martin, the judge from Southport, produced for my inspection a short-legged, prick eared, foxy-faced little black and tan fellow, and did something to whet my curiosity regarding this breed, which is found in considerable numbers around Preston, Ormskirk, the Fylde and district. The Lancashire Heeler looks more like a miniature smooth coated black and tan Corgi than anything else, and there seems little doubt that he is descended from Welsh ancestors. His expression greatly resembles the sharp, intelligent outlook of the Pembroke Corgi. His forelegs are usually bowed, and his tail is left undocked. His ears are usually upright, but drop-eared specimens do occur and are regarded as acceptable". He goes on to say, "From both Mr James G. Ward of Preston (who has kept Heelers for 30 years) and from Dr T. H. Rigg, Parbold (far famed as a breeder of Dachshunds) I have had valuable data on the breed, and both believe that Dachshund blood has been introduced at some time or other".

This account written only 43 years ago, ties in with a lot of other information, especially the Corgi theory. There may well be Dachshund blood in them too.

However, to date, my findings of actual writings favour the Welsh Corgi most. One of the best descriptions comes from a well-known Pembroke Corgi enthusiast (sadly now dead, or I could have asked her first hand!) namely Miss Eve Forsyth Forrest. In her book on "Welsh Corgis" published 1955, she refers to owning a Lancashire Heeler when she was a little girl, (which by my estimation would have been about the year 1910). She said then, "Thinking that a 'Heeler' would be a new type in our family with our pack of dogs and animals of all sorts, he brought her to us and thus I became nominally possessed of, though really owned by, a genuine Lancashire Heeler, or drover's dog. "Tinker" appeared to be a suitable name for my acquisition: she was very black and very tan, with a lovely head and, to my childish mind, big, kind, twinkling eyes. Her ears were slightly over at the tips, but erect when interested and very expressive in all of their many positions. Since everything co-operative was treated as a horse, "Tinker" was measured and proved to be "three hands and one inch" – that is 13 inches high. She had good straight front legs with plenty of bone, a wonderful "nose" and proved to be an efficient ratter in the quarry from which the house had been built. She soon made friends with all the other animals of which she and I made our daily round and, when Corgis came into my life, I recognised her relationship with them both in appearance and character. I had her until I was 13, and she taught me a great deal."

In another Corgi book, "The Pembroke Corgi Handbook" written by Clifford L. Hubbard (published 1952), more reference is made to the Lancashire Heeler together with a picture of a Heeler called "Togo" owned by Mr A. Ripley and Heelers of this type are still about today. Heelers vary in size. Ellis Garner said at one time they were favoured by poachers when the small ones were preferred to be hidden in a large pocket! Also Ellis said many old farmhouses had fireside chairs with a drawer fitted at the bottom. These drawers were often the places some Heelers slept. Therefore more indication shows smaller size.

It is thought the Heelers Corgi type ancestors used to drive cattle from Wales up to the North West coast of England to Lancashire areas. It is there, it is assumed, it may have been bred to a Manchester type Terrier, which would account for its present day appearance and the hunting, ratting, terrier attributes and yet from the Corgi came the cattle working, heeling characteristics.

Some people think that the Corgi theory is the most likely. Not only with the Heeling characteristics, but there are Tricolour Corgis. These are mostly black with tan markings and have white under their chests, body and on paws. It occasionally happens that some Lancashire Heelers are born with some white on their chest, or under the body, and at times on their paws or tip of paws. If the white is very little it often disappears as the puppy grows, and will not show in later life. But for Show purposes, the only permitted white (if any) is allowed on the chest of a Lancashire Heeler, (and that must be a small amount).

Various accounts differ as to old weights of Heelers, whilst one reference is to "a Corgi type dog, weight about 30lb", another says (from Macdonald Daly's article OUR DOGS, 21.12.1956), "the most sought after specimens are no more than 12lb weight". The old height of 13 inches is mentioned in different accounts. It will also be noticed in quotations mentioned that one account refers to forelegs as "usually bowed" whereas Eve Forsyth-Forrest refers to "good straight front legs". Today this is still so, some have straight fronts, and some are bowed. (One may ask, which is right, or which to be preferred? For this the Heeler Standard should be consulted). (Personally it is my belief, bearing in mind the changes recorded by my other breed Pembroke Welsh Corgis, that Heelers may well follow the same pattern, and it may be considered to the breed's advantage to aim for somewhat straighter forelegs). (Update 2002 – this is already happening, over the last 20 years).

It is interesting to look back at old illustrations and photographs of various breeds and see how they have changed over time. The Heeler is already known to have several "types" and winning Heelers whose photographs have appeared prove this. There will always be "types" as in other breeds, but as years go by, and more records are kept, breeding to the Standard should produce less diversity and yet it is hoped the Heeler will not be spoilt by its show requirements and will always maintain its traditional working qualities, even if its history is somewhat enigmatic!

Although documented recorded history may be scarce, and the true development of the Lancashire Heeler as we know it is at the time of writing something of a hazy mystery, we know that this dog has been in parts of Lancashire for generations. What is never in doubt is that it has been kept as a useful Working dog proving its worth in a multitude of ways.

(When first K.C. recognised in 1981 the Lancashire Heeler was classed as a Rare Breed in the Working Group, but was transferred in 1999 to the Pastoral Group. That same year the breed was granted CC status. It is claimed to be the smallest English dog in the Pastoral Group.)

SOME OLD PHOTOGRAPHS OF LANCASHIRE HEELERS

These photos are printed with permission of Mr Ellis Garner, and his mother, Mrs Grace Garner.

This photo was taken over 90 years ago and shows Mrs Grace Garner's mother holding a Lancashire Heeler. The lady beside her is Mr Ellis Garner's Great Grandmother.

(Lancashire Heelers are known to have been kept in this family for at least 160 years.

This photo is 50 years old, and shows Ellis Garner as a boy helping his father on their farm, at hay-making time, and with them one of their Lancashire Heelers.

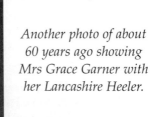

Another photo of about 60 years ago showing Mrs Grace Garner with her Lancashire Heeler.

THE LANCASHIRE HEELER
A Pedigree Dog, 1981

The Lancashire Heeler has been known in some parts of Lancashire and surrounding areas for generations. (To this day not all Lancastrians have heard of the dog bearing their county's name!) Those familiar with it, mostly used it as a working dog, or as family pets and house guards. But outside of the areas named very few knew them. In fact the late Harry Glover listed them among the Extinct Breeds in his "Pure Bred Dogs", first published in 1977. But this was not the case at all.

RECOGNITION IN NORFOLK

Oddly enough, the successful efforts to get this dog recognised as a Pedigree were made in the county of Norfolk. It is thought that at least a couple of attempts had been made before, the last being in the 1940s, with negative results.

Mrs Gwen Mackintosh, who had been interested in dogs all her life, (exhibiting at Crufts in the 1930s and won a Reserve CC with her Standard Dachshund) and who showed various breeds since 1928, took a liking to a Lancashire Heeler when she saw one belonging to a distant relative. Wishing to own one, Mrs Mackintosh advertised in several local papers covering areas in Lancashire and Yorkshire and received a number of replies. Her first one came from a farm on top of a Moor near Clitheroe. Later she bought another, and gradually bred selectively, applying her knowledge and approach of other pedigree dogs. As the years went by Gwen became so fascinated by this attractive, small breed, that she kept quite a number. From time to time there were puppies, and it was quite easy to find suitable homes, as many friends wanted them. Gwen never bred from a commercial angle, her interest was to breed for quality and good specimens. She learned as much as she could about the breed, as there were family homes in Norfolk and Yorkshire, and so was often in the North (as she originated from Halifax). Mrs Gwen Mackintosh was the wife of Mr Eric D. Mackintosh, son of John Mackintosh, the Founder of the well-known Mackintosh's Toffees of Halifax.

Meanwhile the numbers of Lancashire Heelers increased in Norfolk as more people liked and had them, so gradually more breeding resulted, until it was thought how nice it would be to start a Club for them.

CLUB INAUGURATION

The original "Five" who got together to form a Club were Mr Peter and Mrs Pam Welch, Mrs Dolly Rush, Miss Pritt and Miss Jude. This Meeting took place at South Walsham, Norfolk. After the preliminaries, Mrs Gwen Mackintosh was asked to be the Lancashire Heeler Club's President. So a Club was formed, and friendly Meetings took place.

Mrs Mackintosh became quite well known locally at Exemption Shows with her Lancashire Heelers. Her enthusiasm no doubt inspired many others.

It transpired that the late Mr Ben Johnson used to supply Mrs Mackintosh with dog food.

FORMULATING THE BREED STANDARD

Mr Ben Johnson was also an All Rounder judge. He became interested in the Lancashire Heeler breed. He was very helpful with the formulation of the Breed Standard.

After the Club was formed, it was realised that an official Standard should be drawn up. Arrangements were made for a Meeting to be held at Mrs Mackintosh's home, to which all known people interested in Lancashire Heelers were invited to attend and bring with them, their dogs. So people were there from Lancashire and Yorkshire as well, with their dogs. This was on 1st July, 1978. Mr Ben Johnson was there and a Representative of the Kennel Club, Mr Farrand. The various points of the dogs were discussed and considered in great detail. A good representation of types were there. From out of this Meeting, a Standard was formulated, agreeable to all. But after this, the Club circulated to all known owners, asking for any further comments, so any more suggestions could be given fair consideration. This extended to a year. After this opportunity, when it was felt the proposed Standard was acceptable to the majority, the Standard was then submitted to the Kennel Club for consideration. More negotiations followed.

BREED RECOGNITION BY THE KENNEL CLUB

The Kennel Club finally confirmed recognition of the Lancashire Heeler as a Pedigree Dog on 17th July, 1981.

Before K.C. recognition the Club continued to hold its own Shows, some in Norfolk, Yorkshire and Lancashire.

LANCASHIRE HEELER CLUB REGISTERED

The Club was active several years before it was finally approved by the Kennel Club to be registered. This was at the K.C.s Show Regulation Committee on 8th March, 1983.

Mrs Gwen Mackintosh was the Lancashire Heeler Clubs first President, and continued to be so until her death in 1992. She was much respected as the trail-blazer of introducing the Lancashire Heeler into the realms of Pedigree dogs. Her "Acremead" affix was well known, and many of today's Norfolk based Lancashire Heelers (in particular) can be traced back to her original breed lines. From the outset of her keeping the breed, she kept records, so these Pedigrees probably are the most documented.

In 1988, the Lancashire Heeler Club celebrated its Tenth Anniversary (from the time when the Standard was formulated). Up to that time Mr Peter Welch had been Chairman. Mrs Dolly Rush and Mr Peter Welsh were still on the committee.

The first Lancashire Heeler Club Show to be held under Kennel Club Rules was held at Rackheath Village Hall, near Norwich, Norfolk, on 19th May, 1984. The Show Secretary for this was Miss Kathie Kidd, who also ran the ensuing nine KC ruled Shows, held alternately in Norfolk and Lancashire. The Club Membership continues to grow bigger annually, as more people get to know the breed and like to join the Club. There are now members in Finland, (Miss Eeva Lehtinen was our first Overseas Member), Sweden, USA, Holland etc.

As knowledge of the Lancashire Heeler dog has spread, it has kindled interest from many other countries who have asked for more information for their Kennel Clubs, Canine Societies etc., or personal interests. Among these are Finland, Australia, New Zealand, Holland, France, Belgium, USA and Canada. No doubt many others will follow as time passes. Already the Standard has been translated into several other languages, the first was into French, by Dr Delaney who also did an accompanying article for a French Canine Magazine.

In 1996 a Meeting was held to form another Breed Club in the UK to be known as the East of England (proposed) Lancashire Heeler Club. This is unofficial as at time of writing, application to register has not been made, but due to circumstances some people from East Anglia felt the need of another Club. It has proved very popular with organised events and financially successful. Newsletters are sent to Members three times a year.

THE LANCASHIRE HEELER –
A Pedigree Dog 1981

Photo by courtesy of the "Evening News" (Norwich)

This photo was taken in 1978 when the Standard was being considered: From left to right:
Mrs Gwen Mackintosh (Club President); Mrs Dolly Rush (Founder Member); the late Mr Ben Johnson (All rounder judge, who helped to formulate the Lancashire Heeler Standard); Miss A. Jude (Founder Member); Mrs Nesbitt; Mr Peter Welch (Club Chairman); Miss A. Pritt (Founder Member) and Mrs M. Webster.

HOW I GOT MY LANCASHIRE HEELER, 1961
By Mrs Gwen Mackintosh

I first saw a Lancashire Heeler in the garden of a distant relative who had come from Cheshire to live in Norfolk. She said she had had Heelers for many years. I asked her where she had got the present one (who was eight years old) but she had lost the address. I advertised in all the small papers in Yorkshire and Lancashire and got a remarkable number of replies (which unfortunately I only got rid of when I moved three years ago). I finally went up to stay with my father in Halifax and went to some farm on top of a moor near Clitheroe, where there were about five or six who brought in the cattle to be milked. I got my bitch puppy at five and a half weeks old (she wouldn't keep it until it was eight weeks), and eventually came home to Norfolk.

I then started looking for a dog puppy so that I didn't have to chase up to the North to get my bitch mated. I got a lovely little dog from a man who was about 70 then. He had had Heelers all his life and his father before him. He said the gypsies always kept them to keep the goats up with the caravans when they were horse-drawn; and he said pups got dropped off at the various places the gypsies stopped. He also said that before the War (1939) there was a big kennel in Ormskirk, owned by a Lord – (Someone or Other) who was trying to get them recognised by the Kennel Club. This Lord went off to South Africa at the beginning of the War and the Kennel got dispersed. He said that there were some plain Red ones as well as Black and Tan (he thought) but he had never had anything but Black and Tan.

The dog I got for stud never mated my first bitch, but was very prolific with her progeny. I had to take her up North when I wanted her mated. It was difficult to be choosie about the dogs you used as by 1962 or so, they had not always been kept pure. But mine always kept pure till I had to use a dog from Burnham-on-Crouch, who obviously had some white in his make-up, but I think I have got rid of it now.

I have had dogs since I was 19 and showed them quite a lot in my younger days. I have seven Heelers at the moment, the eldest boy being 15 years old. They are very good house dogs and wonderful hunters and as a pack use their heads in catching rabbits etc. Mine are not very well trained for Shows as they rarely go on leads, and walks are taken every day over parkland and woods, running free.

EDITORS NOTE: Mrs Gwen Mackintosh has been showing dogs since 1928. She was President of the Halifax Canine Association. Now is a Life Vice President of the Norfolk & Norwich Canine Society.

(Originally first written in 1989 in "The First Book of the Lancashire Heeler"), Mrs Gwen Mackintosh died in July 1992.

HOW I GOT MY LANCASHIRE HEELER, 1961

*Weather-vane which was on
the roof of Gwens house.*

(Photo by: K.B. KIDD)

*The late President of the
Lancashire Heeler Club,
Mrs Gwen Mackintosh, pictured in
her garden with some of her Heelers in 1977.
Standing in typical stance on the wall is
Acremead Bogey (who lived to be 16)
and was sire of many Heelers.
His great-great grandsire
Acremead Cracker was the father of
Acremead Crisp and Crusty who
were exported to Chicago, USA in 1964.*

In 1965 Acremead Angus also went to Chicago.

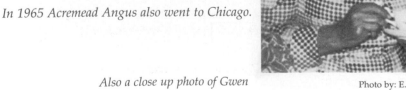

Also a close up photo of Gwen

Photo by: E. M. LEHTINEN

38

Tea, after Lancashire Heeler Committee Meeting held in President's House, Mrs Gwen Mackintosh. Left to right: Mrs Barbara Kidd, Gwen, Miss Eeva M. Lehtinen, Mr Rodney Aldrich.

(Photo by: E.M. LEHTINEN)

Left to right: Kathie Kidd (Show Secretary), Peter Welch (Chairman) seated; Rodney Aldrich (Treasurer) and Gladys Lowe (Secretary). Year was 1985.

(Photo by: K.B. KIDD)

SHOWING A LANCASHIRE HEELER

Dogs walk on handler's left: dog always nearest the judge. Now that more Heelers are appearing in Show Rings, for those who are new to the Show scene, maybe the following would be helpful.

A Heeler is shown on a loose lead. That is the dog stands on the ground and the only contact the handler has, is via the lead. This lead should appear loose with a slight sag in it. It should not appear tight, nor should the dog appear "strung up" by the lead. With training, the dog should stand still and look at its handler, the handler standing facing the dog's head. There should be a little space between handler and dog, so that the judge can quite clearly see the dog in profile. The art is for the handler to keep the dog's attention, without disturbing any other handler or dog in the class. This can be done in a variety of ways, the most common is to have a tit-bit in the handler's hand for the dog to be interested in. Not all dogs will show for food, so it is up to the handler to whisper very quietly, and try to keep the attention that way (not making a noise for anyone else to hear!) (Never use squeaky toys or large bones – these cause too much attention, and are frowned upon by others!) If the dog is too close, never kick the dog. The dog must be re-positioned by using the lead only; not pushed into position with the foot. The dog should stand so that judge can see the outline of the entire head and body. (Not head facing judge or rear end facing judge). A Heeler should stand (like a table) with a leg at each corner, (i.e. four square). Both forefeet and hindfeet should appear in a line (from judges viewpoint) not standing as a GSD would. Do not allow the dog to have its hind and forefeet too close together to make an overall hunched up (arched) back appearance; and similarly do not spread the feet too far apart, to cause the illusion of a dipped topline. Let the dog stand as naturally as it can to appear comfortable and show the body to its best advantage. Do not get on to the floor (ground) and hold the dog in position. Some breeds do, but the Heeler has to be freestanding. (Each breed has its own mode of Showing).

The Heeler is a table dog (i.e. the judge makes his inspection on a table). The handler should stand in front of, but to the side of the dog, holding the lead and not allowing it to dangle untidily about. The handler may at this stage, lightly hold the dog about the neck, to steady it by hand, just to avoid a sudden jump off the table. The dog should be positioned four square again, and prepared in a comfortable position by placing legs with the hands, ready for the judge to assess. (NEVER HOLD THE DOGS TAIL AT ALL, and DO NOT STRING THE DOG'S NECK UP WITH A TIGHTLY HELD LEAD. The only part that should be touched by human hands is the neck only whilst showing on the table. There is no point in holding a Lancashire Heelers tail up whatsoever, as the Lancashire Heeler can hold its tail naturally as it pleases which is down, or if alerted, the dog often holds it over back. This pastoral dog should not be handled like a Terrier). Again the judge must see the complete profile. When the judge has stood back and looked at the profile, he will then come to head of dog, and stand by side of handler to view the head and teeth. At this point, if the handler wishes, if the dog lays its ears right back, the handler may gently cup his hands under front of neck, and just gently use the fingers at back of ears, to assist the judge to see how ears would normally appear. But it is better if dog can be trained to use its ears on its own to give the alert lift required for expression. Apart from that, the handler does not touch the dog when showing, all control must be through the lead and by mutual under-standing (which really will come from training at home and going to Ringcraft Classes). The judge will possibly ask the age of the dog. If the judge speaks to you or asks a question, you may answer, but do not hold a lengthy conversation with the judge, or tell him how good your dog is and how much winning it has done etc. or its general history. Judges make up their own minds of what is before them on the day and assess how the dog is on that day. A dog can win one day, and through poor showing can go away cardless the next. The judge may open the dogs mouth to inspect teeth (the bite) or it is popular these days for hygiene reasons for handler to be asked to open dogs mouth. Do not yank the mouth wide open, all the judge wants to see is the bite, which means a gentle open to reveal the front and along the jaw sides. After judges examination he may say "Do a triangle" – walk a triangle and do walk in a straight line, do not zig-zag, use all space you can so the judge has a chance to assess movement from various angles. When returning to judge, finish by allowing dog to stand still and alerting its attention again. Training at home or Ringcraft lessons should help a lot, it is better to make it 10 minutes a day regularly rather than long boring sessions. A dog which shows well, stands a much better chance of winning. If a dog keeps moving or turning around, it's very difficult for a judge to appraise its true merit. It can happen that a poorer specimen of a dog can win over a really good dog, if it will show well, whilst the really good dog is pulling round in circles and will not keep still. It is not always the dog's fault, there is quite a lot for a good handler to learn about conducting his or her own procedure in the ring. Good handlers must have patience, a lot of it, they must learn to control themselves before controlling the dog. Getting angry with a dog does not improve matters, it makes a nervous dog more nervous. It is often said that a highly nervous handler passes his own emotions down the lead to the dog. A handler with a stable temperament and ready to understand his dog and use gentle persuasion is more likely to have a steady dog in the Ring. When training a puppy for show, it should get the idea that doing what his handler wants is pleasurable, and with praise when it does things right, it will (hopefully!) come to enjoy its training sessions. Too much scolding or smacking a dog (which should not be done anyway) can produce a cringing, shivering dog which will be frightened and so will now not show at its best, as it will be in an unhappy state of mind about the whole thing.

Sometimes when two dogs are almost equal in merit, the final analysis of a judges decision, may well be in favour of the best handling, so there are times when handling by the handler is the difference between winning or losing. This is more likely to be for the highest honours too, when two really good dogs meet to challenge. So Ring Etiquette becomes of paramount importance eventually. It is also a fact that really good handlers can to some extent show a dog to such advantage, that certain faults may be hard to detect by the judge, as the dog is showing so well. It can be said that the dogs matter more than the handling, but as Dog Showing is really a glorified beauty competition, when some dogs look so good, then ring presence has to be considered. This, in the judges language, would come under "Style". There are five essentials in the judges vocabulary which are: Type, Balance, Style, Soundness and Condition.

The **Type** and Breed Character relate to each Breed's Stamp as its Standard asks for.

Balance is a word used for dogs, meaning proportion. A well balanced dog pleases the eye by its features being in correct relation to each other, and a nicely proportioned appearance which instantly appeals by its look of "rightness". Balance is a terrific asset to a show dog. Balance almost instantly "fills the eye" (which means the dog instantly presents an image of what is required and draws the judges attention, to consider further the points it makes on impact).

Style includes Balance, Carriage, Personality and Showmanship. A dog with Style has an alertness which is appealing, attractive and there is an air of pride and eagerness about the dog.

Soundness is mostly used to describe the manner in which dogs move (gait); a good mover would be a "Sound dog", free from disability, and a dog which moves correctly according to its Standard requirements.

Condition is obvious. Dog is in good health, being not too thin or too fat, but having the right amount of covering. Their eyes are bright and sparkle. Coat is looking its best and shows good grooming and is of course clean.

And all the above is expected to apply to a Heeler – a Pastoral Dog! Yes, this is what showing is all about, presenting a dog to look its best. In fact a Heeler is among the easiest to prepare for a Show. Against some other breeds, the Heelers coat is so easy and quick to present.

Sometimes we win, sometimes we don't. There is an art in being a good loser, not to chastise the dog, and to try to accept defeat gracefully and to adopt the attitude, there will be another show, another day and another judge. It is good sportsmanship to congratulate the winners and for high honours shake hands in the ring. Never show bad sportsmanship in the Ring by resorting to tearing up Card or blaming the dog for not winning. **Remember bad behaviour can be reported to the Kennel Club,** and they in turn, have the **power to impose fines if they so wish, or meter out various penalties**.

When showing a dog in the Ring, if possible, always give yourself and your dog enough room, and remember to consider the next person and dog too that they have enough room. Do not walk back and disturb the dog behind you, and do not keep pulling your dog about so as to disturb the next dog. Consider others as you hope they will consider you. Good Luck!

SHOWING A LANCASHIRE HEELER. THE RIGHT AND WRONG WAYS

THE RIGHT WAY TO SHOW A LANCASHIRE HEELER (on the ground)

Photo by: E.M. LEHTINEN

On the ground, control is via the lead only. Note that the dog is free standing.Note that the lead appears to be slack and the human hand is held low. There is no tight lead, no stringing up the dog's head. Handler's hand is close to own body, not held up in the air which often creates a taut, tight lead, making the dog look uncomfortable. This dog looks comfortable. Its attention is drawn to handler the whole time (perhaps with a favourite tit-bit). The judge can easily assess the outline and points of this dog.

THE WRONG WAY TO SHOW A LANCASHIRE HEELER (on the ground)

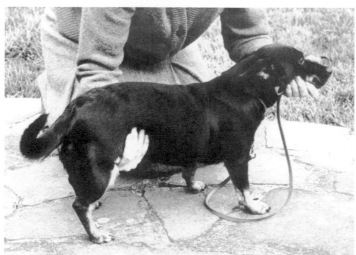

Handler should NOT be down on the ground, but should be STANDING up. Dog should be FREE STANDING without any human hands touching it. Control should be by lead only. Note how human hands spoil the outline. Dog does not look comfortable. Note the lead is untidy on the ground. Because of posture of dog, the judge does not see it to its best advantage.

SHOWING A LANCASHIRE HEELER. THE RIGHT AND WRONG WAYS

THE RIGHT WAY TO SHOW A LANCASHIRE HEELER (on the table)

Note the handler stands in FRONT of the dog, getting its attention. Human hand used at neck to steady the dog. Dog appears comfortable. A clear outline can be seen permitting the judge to easily assess points, thus allowing the dog better consideration.

THE WRONG WAY TO SHOW A LANCASHIRE HEELER (on the table)

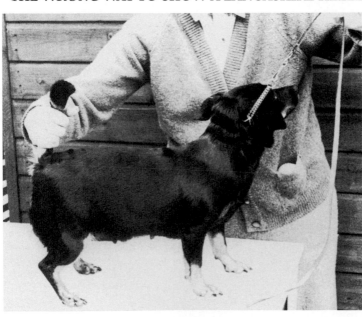

Handler should NOT be behind the dog. Handler should be in FRONT, so dogs attention is drawn forwards. Note here judge does not see a clear profile of head. Wrong to hold tail. (Tail holding could be hiding a fault). Wrong to string-up the head. These wrong things spoil overall outline. Dog does not look comfortable. Wrong handling does not show a dog to its best advantage.

A WORD CONCERNING PERSONAL CLOTHING.

Looking smart probably compliments the dog, but wear comfortable, practical shoes. You may be on your feet for several hours! High heels for ladies are not a good idea, as heels can get stuck in an outside ring's soft ground. Avoid wearing clothes that may "float" in a breeze (e.g. voluminous dresses, long flowing scarves). Equally large, floppy hats can be a nuisance when handling in a Ring. Some heavy ornamental jewellery can also be a distraction if it clinks or clunks!

A little effort to look neat and tidy oneself is a good idea. After all the dog is expected to look its best, and if photographs are taken it is important to record the event looking smart.

Perhaps some attention should be given to clothes colour. Remember Lancashire Heelers are small and either mostly black or liver. Therefore a black dog against black trousers or a liver one against brown trousers will tend to merge, being of one basic colour. A sharper outline is often enhanced by a contrasting background which can make it easier for some judges in a big ring to assess immediately, either in brilliant sunshine or dim lighting conditions, (.e.g. a Marquee exposed to a thunderstorm or torrential rain! It has happened!).

THE LANCASHIRE HEELER
BREED STANDARD

GENERAL APPEARANCE:
Small, powerful, sturdily built, alert, energetic worker.

CHARACTERISTICS:
Works cattle well, but has terrier instincts when rabbiting and ratting.

TEMPERAMENT:
Courageous, happy, affectionate to owner.

HEAD & SKULL:
In proportion to body. Skull flat and wide between ears, tapering towards the eyes which are set wide apart. Moderate stop, equidistant between nose and occiput. Tapering continues towards nose. Skull and muzzle to be on parallel planes.

EYES:
Almond-shaped, medium size, dark colour, except in liver where they may be lighter to match coat colour.

EARS:
Showing alert lift, or erect. Drop ears showing no lift are undesirable.

MOUTH:
Lips firm scissor bite, jaws strong with a regular and complete scissor bite, i.e. upper teeth closely overlapping lower teeth and set square to jaws. Under or overshot to be discouraged.

NECK:
Moderate length, well laid into shoulders.

FOREQUARTERS:
Well laid shoulder, elbows firm against ribs. Amply boned. Pasterns allow feet to turn slightly outwards, but not enough to cause weakness or affect freedom of movement.

BODY:
Well sprung ribbing, extending well back with close coupling. Firm level topline, never dipping at withers or falling at croup. Approximately 2.5 cm (1 inch) longer than height at withers. (Measured from withers to set of the tail).

HINDQUARTERS:

Muscular, with well turned stifles, hocks well let down. From rear should be parallel, when moving or standing. Never bandy or cowhocked.

FEET:

Small firm and well padded.

TAIL:

Set on high, left natural. Carried over back in a slight curve when alert, but not forming a complete ring.

GAIT/MOVEMENT:

Smart and brisk. Natural free movement.

COAT:

Fine undercoat is covered throughout by weather resistant, short, thick, hard, flat topcoat. Topcoat slightly longer on neck. Undercoat should not show through topcoat nor allow any longer hair at the mane to stand off. Long or excessively wavy coat highly undesirable.

COLOUR:

Black or liver with rich tan markings on muzzle, spots on cheeks and often above eyes, from knees downwards with desirable thumb-mark above feet, inside hindlegs and under tail*. Richness of tan may fade with age. White to be discouraged, except for a very small spot on forechest being permitted, but not desired. Pigmentation to tone with coat colour.

SIZE:

Ideal height at shoulder: dogs 30 cms (12 ins); bitches 25 cms (10 ins).

FAULTS:

Any departure from the foregoing points should be considered a fault and the seriousness with which the fault should be regarded should be in exact proportion to its degree.

NOTE: Male animals should have two apparently normal testicles fully descended into the scrotum.

*Note - * (asterisk) at "under tail" refers to colour tan (NOT thumb-mark under tail!). – Editors Note:*

THE LANCASHIRE HEELER - "AT A GLANCE IN BRIEF" POINTS TO LOOK FOR

Refer to Standard

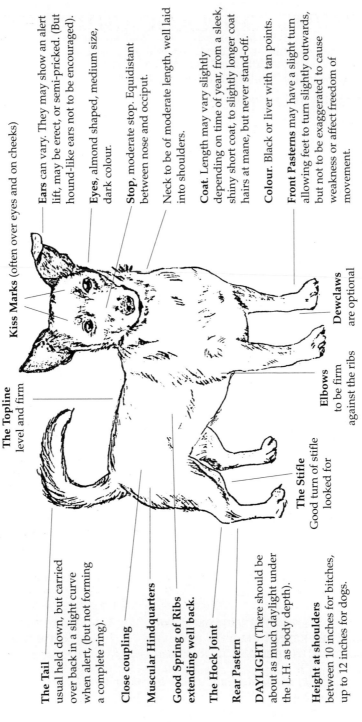

Kiss Marks (often over eyes and on cheeks)

Ears can vary. They may show an alert lift, may be erect, or semi-pricked. (But hound-like ears not to be encouraged).

Eyes, almond shaped, medium size, dark colour.

Stop, moderate stop. Equidistant between nose and occiput.

Neck to be of moderate length, well laid into shoulders.

Coat. Length may vary slightly depending on time of year, from a sleek, shiny short coat, to slightly longer coat hairs at mane, but never stand-off.

Colour. Black or liver with tan points.

Front Pasterns may have a slight turn allowing feet to turn slightly outwards, but not to be exaggerated to cause weakness or affect freedom of movement.

The Topline level and firm

Dewclaws are optional

Elbows to be firm against the ribs

The Stifle Good turn of stifle looked for

The Tail usual held down, but carried over back in a slight curve when alert, (but not forming a complete ring).

Close coupling

Muscular Hindquarters

Good Spring of Ribs extending well back.

The Hock Joint

Rear Pastern

DAYLIGHT (There should be about as much daylight under the L.H. as body depth).

Height at shoulders between 10 inches for bitches, up to 12 inches for dogs.

Drawing by courtesy of Eeva Maija Lehtinen   Captions by K.B.K.   Not to be reproduced without permission.

JUDGING THE LANCASHIRE HEELER

Many times the question has been asked, "What are we looking for, when judging Lancashire Heelers in the Show Ring?"

Firstly, although small, it is a working Dog in the Pastoral Group, so should be shown and handled like one, which is natural. Free standing on the ground, control by the lead only. (Not strung up, not stacked or held). Dog is examined on a table. The dog's head facing the handler at table end. The handler should only touch the dog to steady it, around its neck, preferably with hands under dogs throat, and the fingers can then (if needed) gently support the ears if they have been put flat down. But often many dogs don't need this, they will and can show that alert lift of the ears. No other part of the dog should require human hands, and certainly no stringing up of the head, and no holding up the tail. The dog is so small, from a judging viewpoint, its true outline is seen far better without distractions of human hands pushing or prodding the dog into an "artificial" pose. A judge, worth his (or her) salt, should be able to assess the dog standing naturally much better. (Furthermore, human hands can hide faults!)

JUDGING TO THE STANDARD

As with judging all breeds, the first necessity is to have read, studied and learned thoroughly, the Breed Standard, and have learned as much as possible about the breed before accepting an invitation to judge. (Sometimes it is painfully obvious when a judge has omitted to do this!) And "putting up" types contrary to the Standard is what could bring about the demise of this (at present) "unspoiled by Showing" breed. If a dog happens to be a good showman, and not to Standard in type or size, judges really must look again and think what effect their decisions might have on the breed, if they opt for just a dog showing well, if essentially it falls very short of what the Standard requires. Size, especially must be watched, it is important that this breed should not follow the trend of the Pembroke Corgi, which over the years has become heftier and much lower to ground than old photos of their ancestors show. If much bigger types are "put up" it appears the Lancashire Heeler (as we know it now) might easily become a bigger dog, with far less daylight under it. It would seem a pity if that happened, as it is its small size, but its great characteristics that must surely hold the charm for many an owner. Also small as it is, it can be so agile and some are capable of jumping very high.

HEIGHT

The Lancashire Heeler should be typical of its breed. The height should be between 10 inches (for bitches) and up to 12 inches (for dogs). The current Standard must be adhered to if the desired size is to be preserved.

DAYLIGHT

The ratio of body depth and leg height should be about equal. There should be about as much daylight under the Lancashire Heeler body, as body above it. It should not be a thick, heavy body on short stumpy legs, nor a very thin, long body on longer legs. Body depth and leg height should be equally balanced.

(The outline of a Lancashire Heeler should not look like a Corgi, a Dachshund, a Parson Russell, a Staffordshire Bull Terrier or a Chihuahua [but over the years, at times, resemblances of these have appeared!]). If these untypical specimens were to be "put up", it could entice their happy winning owners, to breed on, or collect Stud Fees, albeit from innocent ignorance, or blatant disregard of the desired Standard type.

COLOUR

The coat colour for Showing is black with tan (preferably rich tan) or liver and tan, tan markings on the muzzle, spots on cheeks and often above eyes (known as "Kiss Marks"). Note the Standard says "often above eyes". Not all Lancashire Heelers have Kiss Marks above the eyes, but this is permitted). The tan to be also from the knees downwards to the feet, with desirable thumbmarks above feet. (Whilst thumbmarks are desirable, not all Lancashire Heelers have them, and lack of them should not debar an otherwise very nice specimen from winning well. Since the breed is still aiming for good conformation and movement, lack of thumbmarks (in my opinion) should only be used as a hair-splitting criteria if in every other way, two very good dogs were of equal merit). Tan is also inside hindlegs and under tail. Tan is also very often inside the ears, but the Standard does not mention this. Some tan may also be across front of chest. Richness of tan may fade with age. If judging older dogs, this should be remembered and allowed for. Whilst a rich mahogany tan is considered very desirable, not all tans are so dark, in fact some are almost sandy coloured. There is a desire to attain and retain the mahogany colouring. Some lines possess it more than others.

Black with tan, or liver and tan markings are the permitted colours for Showing. Any white which may appear is to be discouraged, excepting for a very small spot on forechest being permitted, but not desired. (Sometimes at birth, some puppies are born with a little white on their paws [usually the digits] and sometimes a few white hairs under their chest, but often as the puppies grow these few white hairs will completely go, and after a few months, no trace of white is seen). Where the coat should be black, it should be black and appear to be so! It is not typical for large patches of a chocolate brown to be visible on top.

COAT TEXTURE

The coat texture should be sleek and shiny and smooth. The length may vary slightly depending on the time of year, when the hair at the mane may be slightly longer than the rest of body coat. But the coat of a Lancashire Heeler should not be as thick or as long or as dense as that of a Corgi. A few Lancashire Heelers have been known to have very thick overdone and longer coats causing a coarse appearance on this small dog. Some have had double coats likened to that of a Corgi. (The correct texture of a Lancashire Heeler coat is often regarded as one of the dog's advantages, as it does not shed profusely to make using the Hoover a necessity often around the house). A rough idea of the length of Lancashire Heeler hair is about toothbrush length, (but a little longer at mane).

EXAMINATION ON TABLE

Looking at the dog on the table, the topline should be level, and this is important. The set on of the tail is high. (This means where the root of the tail joins the hindquarters. It does NOT mean an upright tail!) For showing the dog can please itself whether it holds its tail up or down. All that the judge needs to ascertain is the placement of set on. Tails should not be too thick, nor should the rather long hairs on tail be of such a length as to resemble "feathering". Some tails have a few of the tan hairs on the underside. When down, tails should appear black or liver only. Tails are left natural and NEVER docked. Tail lengths vary slightly, but in the down position, most reach to the point of hock. (Not too much emphasis is placed on the tail, apart from the set on, and very important is that the tail should NOT form a complete ring, which might resemble a Pug tail). When alerted the tail is often carried over back in a slight curve.

THE HEAD

The head should be in proportion to the body. The skull and muzzle to be on parallel planes. A moderate but defined stop, with equidistance between nose and occiput. Whilst the Standard says "Skull flat and wide between ears, tapering towards eye which are set wide apart"; this does not mean that the skull should be so broad as to resemble that of a Staffordshire Bull Terrier! As the Standard says, the Skull (at the forehead part) should taper with a proportionate refinement about it. Nose Black on black coated dogs but on liver the pigmentation may be brown or fawn. The Standard says pigmentation to tone with coat colour.

The eyes should be medium sized, of almond shape, and dark brown in colour.

The teeth should have a scissor bite. The lips to be firm. (Obviously undershot or overshot mouths to be discouraged).

Whiskers to be left natural.

EARS

Ears can be erect, or show an alert lift. Those familiar with the breed can see directly if they comply to Standard or not. (Except to ascertain that there is an alert lift, it is not really necessary to throw objects or wave hankies to see the dog use its ears). The type of ear which is not desirable for showing is the drop ear which hangs down seemingly lifeless (the original Standard referred to a Houndlike ear being undesirable). Some puppies ears attain the desired position early (about 5 months) whilst others may take about 9 months or even a little longer. Therefore, when judging, this should be remembered and in some cases allowances made.

THE BODY

Neck should be of moderate length and well laid into shoulder. The fore-quarters should have elbows firm against the ribs. Elbows should not stick out, or be loose. (A young puppy not fully mature might have "loose elbows" which could tighten correctly as it grows). But as the Standard says "firm against the ribs" is wanted. Body should have well sprung ribbing, extending well back with a close coupling. Looking at the dog from the front, the pasterns may allow the feet to turn slightly outwards, but not enough to cause weakness or affect freedom of movement. (A few years back a number had very poor fronts, but they are improving. Whilst the pasterns may allow the feet to turn slightly outwards, there were specimens where this was so exaggerated, that many had what were known as Queen Anne, Chippendale or Fiddle Fronts. This, therefore, contributed to some very poor movement). More recently this has improved, but when judging, these fronts need to be carefully considered, as some dogs may look good standing, but when walking "fall apart" (their movement is very poor). Those with better fronts also can move better. When assessing the pasterns, it is important to consider the bone structure and not be affected by optical illusions of colour markings which may go down the forearm and end in the area of the carpal joint. It is often the shape of the black

52

colour merging with the tan that can give a false impression making a pastern turn look worse than permitted. But it is up to the judge to notice the difference. The feet should be small, firm and well padded.

DEWCLAWS

The Standard does not mention dewclaws but these are optional. Any hind dewclaws should have been removed. Some breeders leave front dewclaws on, whilst others prefer (for safety reasons) to have them removed when puppies are very young, as is the custom with most other breeds. With or without front dewclaws should not affect the overall judging of the dog.

MOVEMENT

Movement is a very important aspect when judging. It is necessary for a judge to be able to differentiate between the various gaits, particularly with Lancashire Heelers. There may be as many as half a dozen or so who look good standing still showing in the Ring, but when each one is moved, then some glaring differences can show up, as to how they walk! As this dog is so small, some judges feel they get better advantage by stooping themselves to see better at ground level. I am inclined to agree with this. Watching dogs from the angle of a ringside viewer gives a different impression of the angle from which a judge can see the dog move. He or she can see it coming straight on, or going, and this tells more than the side angle. One is able to see how the feet are lifted – and there are lots of ways of doing this! The way a Lancashire Heeler should move is smart and brisk, with a natural free movement. (But over the years some Lancashire Heelers have been seen to be winging, paddling, toeing-in, daisy clipping, plaiting, having hackney action to name but a few!)

The hindquarters should be muscular, with Hocks well let down. From the rear should be parallel, when moving or standing, and not be bandy or cow hocked. There should also be a good turn of stifle. Again the rear movement needs to be watched, but in general, more Lancashire Heelers (currently) have better hind movement than front movement.

WEIGHT

The weight is not given in the Standard, and this varies rather according to type. Some are about 9 lbs up to about 17 lbs. if of the heftier type. Most would come between these weights.

THE TEMPERAMENT

Is happy and affectionate to owner.

SOME FAULTS AND CORRECT POINTS

| SKULL AND MUZZLE NOT ON PARALLEL PLANES | LACK OF STOP SNIPEY | DOMED SKULL SHORT MUZZLE | CORRECT PROPORTIONS |

| EYES TOO BULBOUS AND WRONG SHAPE | EYES TOO SMALL | JOWLY-LOW SET EYES | CORRECT EYE PLACEMENT AND SIZE |

ACCEPTABLE TAIL CARRIAGE

WRONG – THIS FORMS A COMPLETE RING.

| COW HOCKED | BANDY (OPEN HOCKED) | CORRECT, PARALLEL HOCKS |

| SPLAY FEET (OPEN TOES) | CLOSE, LOW HOCKS | HARE FEET | CORRECT FOREFEET |

TOPLINES SHOWING SOME FAULTS and the Correct Topline

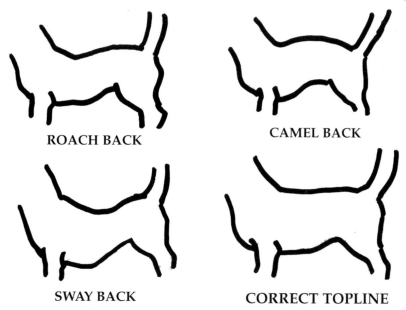

ROACH BACK   CAMEL BACK

SWAY BACK   CORRECT TOPLINE

THE TAIL CARRIAGE OF LANCASHIRE HEELERS

Photo by: K.B. KIDD

This photograph shows typically the way in which Lancashire Heelers will hold their tails. When alerted, the tail curves over back (but should not be in a tight ring). Or the tail is often carried down naturally. (Either way is acceptable for showing).

THE VARIOUS EAR SETS OF LANCASHIRE HEELERS

*These drawings show the various
Ear Sets complying to Standard,
"showing alert lift or erect".
(For showing Houndlike ears
are not to be encouraged).*

*Above is a young puppy head
before ears show any lift.*

Drawings by E.M. Lehtinen.

Copyright 1988

OUTLOOK ON JUDGING
And Thoughts for Those Wanting to Start

There is (or should be!) more to judging than just standing in the middle of a Ring and selecting three or five dogs out of any given number! Although that is how it looks – too easy! Experienced judges, worthy to be called such, know differently.

LEARNING

Some people when they leave school, think that is the time to stop learning. But most things in life qualify for "One is never too old to learn". Surely in the Show world of dogs, there can be no end to learning? So those aspiring to judge should go among dogs, talk about dogs, read about dogs and in short learn all they can, including Ring etiquette, the procedure of behaviour etc. There are Kennel Club Rules to be learned. Helping or learning to steward all contributes towards the general outlook as to Ring procedures which need to be observed. Standards must be learned.

EXPERIENCE

Ideally, long experience both practically and from the Pedigree Show in depth study of any given breed should constitute the basis for judging.

But it doesn't always happen that way nowadays. A person who can boast of breeding hundreds of dogs, is not necessarily a good judge. He or she might produce lots of dogs, not with the aim of helping to improve the breed, but only with the aim of selling for profit, and such people would not bother with a word such as "conformation".

Equally, purely academic study is not the answer either.

It is a combination of being with dogs, mixing with dogs and experienced, genuine, reputable dog people and learning from them, but as well, being prepared to make a serious study of the breed (or breeds) concerned, and being able to express just what makes any given dog have the appearance it does, or in how it differs when compared to another or other dogs. Therefore, any further learning which will aid to assess in making good judgement must be helpful.

Years ago serious education for Canine judging did not exist as we know it today. It was all based on "having an eye for a dog" (or "an eye for a horse"). This was all right where it applied truly, but anyone could think they "had an eye", so it was rather hit-and-miss and in some cases might well have depended on the "old pals act" of putting in a good word at the right place for a friend.

FURTHER KNOWLEDGE

For those who want to these days, Canine education exists and many aspects of judging can be learned and applied practically by being "in" dogs or with dogs too. Various lectures, seminars and courses are available and often advertised in the Dog Press, and so can be enjoyed by those wishing to avail themselves of further knowledge concerning dogs. (Since this was originally written, the Kennel Club now requires Breed Clubs to organise certain basic education as well as instructive guidelines for judging, which is a very good thing).

Of course, there are a few people who scorn or pooh-pooh any type of further dog knowledge as something not to be touched with a barge pole! Usually these people are the ones who have not subjected themselves to any formal test or course, as they may feel it was beneath their dignity, or could it be that their scorn may be hiding a fear of failing any such test, and thus losing face?!

SIMILE OF DOG JUDGING AND CAR DRIVING

If a simile is made, perhaps in these modern times dog judging could be considered as car driving. Car driving looks easy, and just told how, anyone can set a car in motion and be steering, one could be said to be "driving". But as car drivers know, there is a lot more to it than that! Years ago, there was no driving test, so much by trial and error motorists evolved. (Originally it did not matter much where the car was driven, as there were so few on the road and road signs were practically non existent in many country lanes). But as time passed, more and more cars came on the roads, so it became necessary to have driving tests, so that the right signs were understood and obeyed, that traffic was conducted in an orderly fashion. With the Driving Test, drivers have to prove that they know how to control the car, what they are doing and why. Experienced car drivers are having to make decisions the whole time, sometimes split second decisions, and they have to be right! With so many vehicles now on motorways, the standard of driving and learning more has to be much higher than it was on those country lanes years ago, which probably had only two cars on them per day!

So is it slowly happening with Dog Judging? With more exhibitors going to shows than ever before, with more dogs to be judged, and more money being paid out for the events, it is getting like the motorways where a higher standard of capability for the job is expected. When exhibitors pay several pounds to enter classes at Championship Shows (or some Open Shows are getting expensive too) surely they are entitled to a judge who has done everything possible to base his, or her decisions on knowledge of the breed and thorough understanding of conformation and movement and knowing the Standard. (Like the driver who knows his Highway Code!)

If road signs are interpreted wrongly, so a bad result can happen – even an accident.

Similarly, experienced judges are interpreting signs of what they see and feel, and assessing the signs correctly produces a good result. This should help the breed in the long run, and should be seen to be fair to Exhibitors.

The message here, if wanting to start to judge dogs, is not only to have kept or bred them for some years but to learn as much as possible by any means possible; talking to experienced people; mixing with dogs; reading about judging procedures in many books on the subject (often available free from libraries); attending any courses or lecturers, teach-ins etc; watching canine films, (often shown at lectures etc).

Currently one of the leading courses on Dog judging is run by the Canine Studies Institute. This goes on for about 7 months or longer, but the vast majority of those who took it and passed felt they had benefited from it, and the necessary hours of study had widened their horizons. Those who achieved the Diploma had to work for it, it was not handed out easily. (Incidentally, before anyone can take this particular course the prospective student's suitability is considered as to whether or not they would be accepted).

It used to be the case in most breeds that before one could even dream of aspiring to a first judging appointment that an "apprenticeship" was served. This in effect, was usually a period of 5 or 7 years being in the breed and actively showing, during which time it was felt that some knowledge of the breed would have been gained. This was a good thing, as this also gave a newcomer time to have a few ups and downs with winning and losing and time to learn sportsmanship. But these days it sometimes happens that a person who has never shown before, might be lucky and win at the outset several times with a good dog that they bought not by judgement, but by chance luck, and the fact that they started winning when the whole show scene was new to them, appears to go to their head and within a very short period of time, they adopt the attitude that "they know it all", and immediately think they should become a judge. (Referring back a few paragraphs, this is rather like the learner car driver behind a wheel on a motorway who hasn't learned the Highway Code and can't interpret the road signs!!)

It seems rather odd that whilst the United Kingdom reputedly has some of the best dogs in the World, when it comes to educating aspiring judges, some other Continental countries and the USA seem far ahead.

The Kennel Club has become more particular about judges knowledge over the past few years and encourages more learning.

CRITIQUE
After the show, a judge is expected to write a Critique on the winning dogs which he (or she) judged. This should be done very soon after the Show, and sent to both canine newspapers which publish show results. Many exhibitors eagerly await to read the judge's opinion and comments on dogs which won at Shows. If Critiques are not made or published, it is often a disappointment.

TETANUS INJECTION
Some people who go among dogs a lot, or do judging where they will be handling a lot of strange dogs, think that to have a Tetanus injection is wise. This is entirely up to the individual, who in the event, should consult their doctor about it. (Note: It is sometimes found that a few people are allergic to the injection).

FURTHERING EDUCATION ABOUT DOGS

In recent years the Kennel Club has been becoming keener that the Dog showing fraternity are aware of Show Regulations, Ring Procedures and the practical aspects of judging, also to provide training on Canine conformation and movement. To this end Breed Clubs and other organisations are asked to run Seminars to further educate breed followers. This involves the Breed Standard points, conformation and characteristics etc., etc., for any chosen breed and all aspects attributed to it.

Therefore both Lancashire Heeler Clubs are complying and these events are usually well attended and popular. Speakers chosen are mostly experienced people who have been interested in the breed for several years or Guest Speakers who may have been invited to talk on specific matters appertaining to health, foods or any current problems relating to the canine world etc. or perhaps guests with particular Veterinary knowledge or from overseas, all of which can be useful information to widen interest and learn.

These events are usually planned for a whole day, often with morning coffee, lunch and afternoon tea provided, which helps towards a pleasant social atmosphere. But at the end of the learning sessions very often a Test is held when marking determines those who qualify to receive a Certificate of attendance which may prove useful towards a C.V. if aspiring to judge, or at least an earned keepsake of satisfaction of a day well spent.

Many Breed Clubs give advance notice of when and where Dog Educating dates will take place through advertisements in the Canine Newspaper or in Members Newsletters.

A SEMINAR TO FURTHER EDUCATION
ABOUT THE LANCASHIRE HEELER

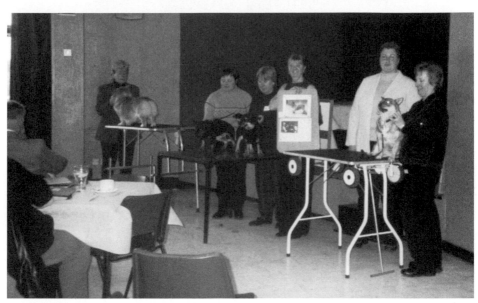

A Lancashire Heeler Seminar organised by the East of England (proposed) Lancashire Heeler Club, showing dogs to illustrate conformation, held February 2002 at Norwich. Pictured are Mrs Carol Mitchell with a Corgi, Mrs Jeanettte Livesey, Miss Jacky Cutler, Mrs Julie Swann with L. Heelers, Miss Sarah Whybrow and Mrs Stella Coombes with a Swedish Vallhund.

Illustrating Points of the Breed Standard being explained here by Mrs Julie Swann (Chairman of the Lancashire Heeler Club) and Miss Jacky Cutler ((Chairman of East of England) (proposed) Lancashire Heeler Club).

FURTHERING EDUCATION ABOUT DOGS

A Seminar with Guest Speaker Mr M.J.R. Stockman, M.R.C.V.S. talking on Anatomy using a dog skeleton, assisted by Jacky Cutler with a Lancashire Heeler and a Keeshond looks on.

Seminar Guest Speakers Miss Kathie Kidd (a former Chairman), Mrs Julie Swann (current Chairman of Lancashire Heeler Club) and Officers of The East of England (proposed) Lancashire Heeler Club, Miss Sarah Whybrow (Secretary), Miss Jacky Cutler (Chair person) and Mrs Stella Coombes (Treasurer).

POINTS OF THE DOG

The Sketch on page 64 is a general impression of a dog to name some of the parts – not specifically a Lancashire Heeler!

THE TOPLINE	is the area from the withers to the base of tail, as seen in profile.
THE HEIGHT	of a dog is measured from withers to ground.
THE LENGTH	of a dog is measured from point of shoulder to point of buttock.
THE STOP	is the depression at the junction of the nose and skull. (More pronounced on some breeds than others).
THE OCCIPUT	is the protruberance at the high point of and at back edge of the skull. (More obvious on some breeds than others).
THE LOIN	is the part between the last rib and the croup.
THE CROUP	is the part of the back from the front of pelvis to root of tail. (The pelvis is part of the croup. A steep croup means a steep pelvis).
COUPLING	is the part of the body between ribs and pelvis.
SET ON OF TAIL	Where the root of tail is set on to hindquarters.
STIFLE	Joint is the equivalent to man's knee joint.
PATELLA	Small bone at stifle joint in rear leg, equivalent to human knee cap.
THE POINT OF HOCK	Corresponds to man's heel. (The "hock" it is important to know, is the joint only (the tarsal bones). Not to be confused with the rear pastern which consists of the metatarsal bones. Some writers refer to "the hocks" when in fact they really mean the rear pasterns).
DEWCLAWS	Fifth digit found on the inside of the legs at birth. In most breeds, removed, being considered undesirable except in a few breeds where they are retained.
	Note: the digits are the bones of the paws so on front paws would be considered equivalent to man's fingers and on rear paws, to man's toes.

POINTS OF THE DOG
NAMING OF THE PARTS TOPOGRAPHICAL ANATOMY
(The dog as we see it. A description of the regions of the body)

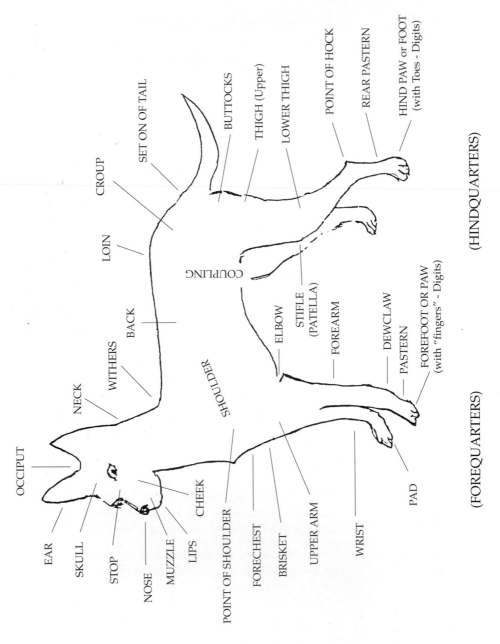

POINTS OF THE DOG IN ENGLISH & FINNISH

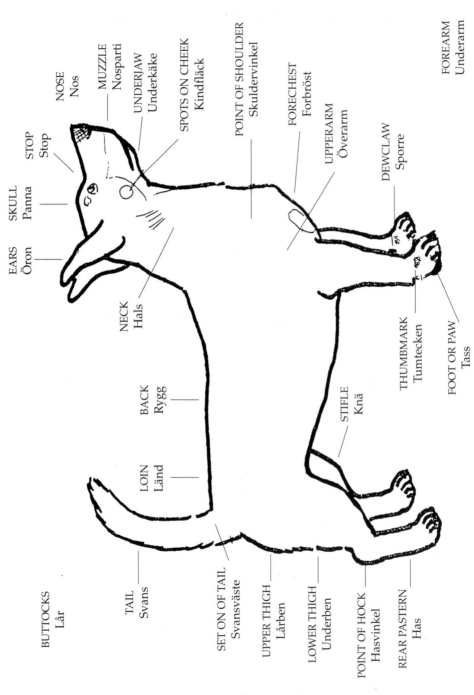

FOREARM
Underarm

MUZZLE
Nosparti

UNDERJAW
Underkäke

SPOTS ON CHEEK
Kindfläck

POINT OF SHOULDER
Skuldervinkel

FORECHEST
Forbröst

UPPERARM
Överarm

DEWCLAW
Sporre

NOSE
Nos

STOP
Stop

SKULL
Panna

EARS
Öron

NECK
Hals

THUMBMARK
Tumtecken

FOOT OR PAW
Tass

BACK
Rygg

STIFLE
Knä

LOIN
Länd

BUTTOCKS
Lår

TAIL
Svans

SET ON OF TAIL
Svansväste

UPPER THIGH
Lårben

LOWER THIGH
Underben

POINT OF HOCK
Hasvinkel

REAR PASTERN
Has

THE FUTURE OF THE LANCASHIRE HEELER

It was amazing that here in the British Isles, an old English breed has survived the test of time, and because of the few people who were dedicated to try to keep the breeding true, we have today this very small, but so versatile dog. Those who have become acquainted with it for the first time, only recently, consider it as something of a novelty. Those in Lancashire and surrounding areas who have kept Lancashire Heelers for generations are to be commended, and those in Norfolk whose efforts made it possible for the dog to be shown and become wider known have contributed jointly to supplying the dog loving fraternity with another small breed hitherto little known countrywide or world-wide for many people to enjoy.

But what of its future?

Will the breed as known today remain thus? After a few years will the Lancashire Heeler still be about the size of a cat but with all of its canine versatile use and characteristics?

EXPOSURE TO THE SHOW SCENE

Or will the introduction of becoming known as a Pedigree dog which inevitably will mean more exposure to the whims of the Show scene fashions, bring about a gradual but noticeable change of the breed's appearance? It is known that some other breeds have gradually altered in appearance because of the chain of events of Showing. At first thought this statement may not seem feasible, but reference to history of some other breeds which have much documentation including many photos and drawings, bears out how the influence of Showing has altered todays dogs from those of their ancestors.

With some affected breeds, it was a change of size, either larger or smaller; or weight change to heavier or lighter; in other cases, coat differences; others, the leg height has slowly changed. For some the head expressions have gradually changed from their ancestors' types.

This seems hard to realise, nevertheless many people who are enthusiasts of breeds where this has happened will understand and acknowledge the fact.

So, if the Lancashire Heeler is to be kept as we know it now 2002, it will be a case of always being vigilant, to be aware when slight change appearances start to regularly reoccur.

BREEDERS AND JUDGES

What happens to the Lancashire Heeler is entirely in the hands of Breeders and Judges.

Both have a considerable degree of influence caused by their decisions. Both **should** have a responsibility to the Breed **to breed to the Standard** and **Judge to the Standard**.

If some judges select untypical specimens (e.g. too big, too much bone, great big heads, coats too heavy etc.) and these are awarded high winning honours, to the uninitiated (Novices) these winning dogs would be thought the best. Then the owner of the dog might be asked for puppies from it and so continue to attempt to breed this particularly "fashionable" specimen on. Equally if a male, the owner might very likely be inclined to advertise it for Stud (and charge a handsome fee, all to his or her benefit). But of no benefit to the actual Breed. So that is how the gradual creep of change could come about. After a few years of progeny deliberately bred to look like the "great Winner" then those types become "fashionable". Again judges not thoroughly acquainted with the breed might continue to award top honours to these! So more could get bred by breeders who may want to be known for producing "winning stock". Eventually the numbers of this "fashionable" type could swamp the original type until it would be hard to find "pure bred" sires or dams still carrying the originally known and liked characteristics.

SUITABILITY OF JUDGES

It is therefore very important when Canine Societies or Breed Clubs select judges that serious consideration should be given to the suitability of a judge. (Judges should be invited who are known to **know the breed**, not who may know a pal or some committee!) Judges should remember that if exhibits are not worthy of merit, they can withhold awards. (Consult current K.C. Rule Book).

It may not make the judge of the day popular with an owner who is denied a withheld Award. It also takes a brave judge to do this. But bearing the long term good of the breed in mind, there will be times when this should be done. When judges really know the breed very well and are themselves experienced, then when exhibits fall very obviously short of the Standard, they should remember K.C. Rule on this, and exercise it.

Because the Lancashire Heeler had been considered "new" to the Show scene, it had been noticed that a few judges have appeared to have been selected at random who did not know the Standard, which does not help the breed, nor is fair to exhibitors.

JUDGING LIST

The Lancashire Heeler Club has a Judging List, and any Canine Society who is in doubt as to choice of Lancashire Heeler Judge, are asked to contact the Lancashire Heeler Club Secretary, to obtain the up-to-date Lancashire Heeler Club appointed Judges. The Kennel Club also has this Judging List. The Lancashire Heeler Club also has its own criteria for those wishing to make applications to be considered for its Judges List. These forms comprise of a number of relevant questions which applicants must complete to be submitted to the Lancashire Heeler Committee for consideration and it will be at their discretion as to whether aspiring applicants satisfy requirements to be admitted to the list or not. This falls into line with other Breed Clubs, who like their Breed Judges to be considered suitable for the responsibility and honour of judging.

SOME JUDGES OBSERVATIONS SINCE 1981

Since some of the first judges who judged Lancashire Heelers (with Pedigree Status since 1981) have again had an opportunity to judge the breed after an interval of a few years, their comments have been that it was noticeable that more uniformity was apparent than on their first appointment. Therefore this signifies that many breeders are trying to breed to the Standard.

When the Breed was first K.C. recognised, among some of the first to make their debut in the show rings were quite a number with very poor general conformation and movement. So, for some time, emphasis was placed on this to aim for much better conformation. This being a major factor. Therefore some of the less important details were considered "icing on the cake" which could be overlooked to some extent where a dog possessed very good conformation and movement. After 21 years of showing conformation in general has improved very much.

As time goes on it becomes more important that judges really know the breed and what they are doing.

THE FUTURE

The future of the breed rests in the hands of those who breed litters and those who select winners at K.C. Ruled Shows.

For better, for worse . . .

We can but hope that this delightful small breed will remain unspoiled . . .

BREEDING FOR QUALITY, NOT QUANTITY

It is greatly hoped that any breeding will be to aim for quality and not quantity. Exploitation of any breed just for human greed or money is deplorable, and inevitably leads to problems for the breed. Any breeding should be approached with the idea to be selective as to matings, and in the knowledge that all the resulting puppies will be wanted by suitable owners. "Puppy Farmers" and "Back Street breeders", have done great injustice to other breeds in the past.

The Kennel Club are aware of what excessive breeding of dogs can do, and that is one of the reasons for introducing the Code of Ethics. All Lancashire Heeler Club Members are asked and expected to abide by the Lancashire Heeler Code of Ethics.

THE FUTURE OF THE LANCASHIRE HEELER
USEFUL INFORMATION

THE KENNEL CLUB, LONDON, CAN SUPPLY MOST INFORMATION ON CANINE MATTERS. THE ADDRESS IS WRITTEN BELOW WHICH MIGHT PROVE HELPFUL.

THE LANCASHIRE HEELER CLUB (approved by the Kennel Club 1983) has continued over the years holding Shows, Fun Days, Seminars, etc. Its numbers fluctuate slightly, but annual averages of Members hover around about 200 (with some from overseas). Membership includes Newsletters (usually two each year) which circulate current affairs. As with all Clubs, periodically Officers and Committee change, therefore so do telephone numbers and addresses needed for contact. For practical reasons and latest updates it seems wiser here to print the Kennel Club's address as they are constantly keeping records, and should be able to advise on Secretary's latest telephone number etc.

> THE KENNEL CLUB
> 1-5 CLARGES STREET, LONDON W1J 8AB, ENGLAND.
> Tel: (as at March 2002) Main Switchboard 0870 6066750

THE LANCASHIRE HEELER RESCUE. There is a rescue service which cares for dogs needing rehoming for various reasons. For more information about this, contact the Lancashire Heeler Club Secretary who can supply details of persons operating it. (Current Telephone Number and address from:

> THE KENNEL CLUB, 1-5 CLARGES STREET, LONDON W1J 8AB.

LANCASHIRE HEELER PRODUCTS. The Club has a Stall at some Shows where many varied items can be bought with the Lancashire Heeler motif on. Or a list of products with prices can be sent for and sent out by post. (Information via the Club Secretary).

SOME HELPFUL ADVICE AND HINTS FOR THOSE STARTING TO SHOW

Having decided that you want to start going to Dog Shows, with your dog, there are certain things to do, or to take, which will be useful.

The first thing to mention here is the keeping of any wins gained in a Show Record Book (or noted on paper, which is kept for future reference). It is quite simple, but as time goes on and as the dog wins more and more, it will become ineligible for certain classes, and when the show schedules are referred to, the total number of wins for certain classes has to be known, so that only those classes still eligible are entered for forthcoming shows. Below is the idea on how to keep a list of wins. (Show Record Books can be bought at various stands at most Championship Shows. Or our Lancashire Heeler Club Secretary may be able to supply).

The width of the double page needs to be at least 10 inches wide. As an example here, the space is narrower than it would be in practice.

SHOW RECORD					
DATE	SHOW	TYPE OF SHOW	JUDGE	CLASS	AWARD

If more than one dog is shown, keep a separate record book for each dog.

When travelling by car to dog shows, most Lancashire Heeler owners like to use a collapsible, easy to assemble, metal mesh dog cage. These give protection to the dog and when wanting to be used at the show to keep the dog in, can be quickly folded to carry in. Various designs and sizes are usually on sale at most Championship Dog Shows, or they can be bought at some pet shops, or sent away for by post.

For normal walking out use, the dog will need a proper **lead** and **collar** with an **identity disc** with its home address and telephone number on. (And for travelling, it should wear this collar and disc in case of accident, when if the dog escaped a finder would know where the dog belonged and be able to return it to its rightful home). Micro-chipping is becoming very popular and getting less expensive. This should be done by a vet or qualified person.

For showing, a **Show Lead** (of lighter weight) is popularly used. (Bought at most dog shows, or pet shops). In the Ring usually **Show Chains** are worn instead of the usual collar. These Show Chains are available in various sizes. Lancashire Heelers need a small and lightweight type. They are either of the slip-chain type or a fixed complete circle which tightness up when worn with the lead attached.

(For Lancashire Heelers it is my personal choice, as I have experienced the single long slip chain type, to let the Lancashire Heelers out of it!) Or there is a nylon type of show lead with collar combined.

Blanket or **cover** for the dog to sit on inside the cage.

Another cloth to cover, if outside and the sun or wind is too fierce. (A dog can suffer stress in hot sun).

Shallow, lightweight plastic **dish** for the dog to drink water from.

Towel to dry dog if needed.

A Ring Card Clip (bought at most dog shows) to hold ring number to attach to own coat to wear in the Ring.

Pen or **Pencil** to mark the winning numbers in the catalogue.

Folding lightweight chair (if wanted, needed at some outside shows).

Small plastic bottle to hold water for dog.

A fold-up, lightweight **Mackintosh** (for the unexpected shower! Plastic or nylon macs are popular).

If a car owner, a pair of **Wellington boots** permanently left ready in car boot, can be so useful, when grass is wet or ground muddy (as it often is!)

A fold up hat is useful, or headsquare when wet or sun too hot.

A thermos flask with own choice of drink in, can be a Godsend, either at the Showground, or to drink in the car after long journeys.

A road map (preferably with a lot of detail on. Ordnance Survey Motoring Atlases are good on a Scale of 3 miles to 1 inch).

A torch for early, dark mornings and nights – often wanted to map read!

A few paper tissues can be handy. (And a plastic bag – in case dog fouls at the wrong spot!)

Very important is a Show Bag. This should have a shoulder strap, so when entering show venue, the hands are free to cope with dogs etc. (Show bag should be lightweight material, to allow more weight for other items going inside it!)

Some people also invest in a large umbrella for times when the sun is too hot at ringsides, but this doesn't happen often!

For those interested, a camera can record events.

CLOTHES for Dog Shows, wear comfortable clothes and especially comfortable shoes. (For ladies high heels are often a hazard, as they stick in the mud and are not comfortable on bumpy mounds of turf). A woolly cardigan is very useful as often the wind blows up.

SAFETY PINS having one or two fairly large safety pins can prove a wonderful salvation! They will serve to pin ring cards, or "rescue" broken zips etc! (Quite often someone is asking for one, when their clothes need holding up in an emergency!)

SOME SUGGESTED READING

"**Showing and Judging Dogs**" by Hilary Harmer (publisher: John Gifford)

"**Gait**" by Rachel Page Elliot. (publisher: Howell Book House)

"**Dog Breeding**" a Guide to Mating and Whelping" by Kay White. (Bartholomew)

"**The Doglopaedia**" (A Complete Guide to Dog Care). J.M. Evans and Kay White. (Henston)

"**The Practical Dog Dictionary**" by Kathy Kidd. (Kelso) (An illustrated Guide to Dog Terms, Definitions & Anatomy, for the Breeder, Shower, Judge and Enthusiast). Available direct from K. Kidd.

"**Don't Panic**" by Wendy Lewis. A Guide to Whelping, Rearing and Selling Puppies. Direct from Mrs W.T. Lewis (featured in this book).

"**The Reluctant Farmer**" by Wendy Lewis (author of "Don't Panic"). For lighter humorous fiction reading, highly amusing about country life with cows, sheep and dogs. Received excellent reviews. Recommended. Available from Booksellers by ordering quoting "The Reluctant Farmer" by Wendy Lewis = ISBN 1-903970-09-1 (Price £8.99).

WEEKLY CANINE NEWSPAPERS

"**Our Dogs**", 5, Oxford Road, Station Approach, Manchester M60 1SX

"**Dog World**", Somerfield House, Wotton Road, Ashford, Kent TN23 6LW

(Available from most Newsagents, or can be ordered or sent by post).

TAR OR OIL ON PAWS

Over the years a number of owners have asked how to remove Tar or Oil from their dogs' paws. This is often the result of melted tar on pavements in hot weather, or nowadays several beaches have spots of oil or tar substances washed up on them. When this gets on and between dogs paws it has to be removed with the minimum of discomfort to the dog, which rules out many chemical solutions. Getting tar or oil off clothes or human skin with branded manufactured removers is quite different from removing tar from a dog who will invariably lick the affected part, and in so doing swallow some of the chemical compound which could be dangerouss.

Having experienced tar and oil hazards from walking our dogs on the beach we found the best form of gentle remover to be margarine for dogs paws! Butter can be used in the same way, but margarine is cheaper, and our experience is that "Stork" brand is the best!

Removing any tar is messy, even using eucalyptus oil for our own clothes or shoes, so using margarine for dogs is no exception!

The method is as follows:

Requirements:

Old Newspapers	Old towel
Lots of paper tissues	Half pound "Stork" margarine
Receptacle for soiled tissues	Bowl of warm soapy water (NOT detergents)

Wherever this job is done ensure that dog is well away from good carpets! It is better to use a room that does not matter because should the dog run about, the mess can quickly transfer where unwanted!

Wear an apron or old clothes yourself.

Spread newspapers on floor. Have the box of paper tissues ready for use. Have the margarine opened ready.

Kneel yourself and lay the dog on his/her back on the newspapers. Using paper tissues wipe off excess tar. When the largest blobs are off, there will be tar between the paws.

Using tissues put generous portions of margarine between the pads (doing one paw at a time). It will be seen that margarine gets well between the pads and helps to dilute the tar/oil substance. Wipe that away. Keep on repeating gently until the tar or oil has gone. This will take patience and a lot of paper tissues!

When all paws are tar/oil free, then one at a time wash paws in warm soapy water (do not use detergent powders). Then dry with an old towel (which may well get more tar residue on it!)

Check all paws thoroughly before allowing dog to run on good carpets.

This may seem a strange method, but it has been very successful for us and when dogs have licked their feet afterwards, there was no unpleasant chemical used – only margarine, which some seemed to enjoy!

PORTRAIT GALLERY

Important Note: In the Portrait Gallery and Advertisement Sections,
the details have been supplied by owners. The authors cannot accept
any responsibility if there might be any inaccuracies.

Photo by: EEVA-MAIJA LEHTINEN

BOWANNE LOLLYPOP LIL

Bitch   Born: 16.2.01

Owner: LILIAN HAKKARAINEN
RAHAPAJANKATU 1 C 11, 00160 HELSINKI, FINLAND
Tel: +358 9 611 575

Breeder: MRS A. C. BOWES

Sire: CAESAR SUMMER SOLSTICE AT BOWANNE	PAPTONS TOP SECRET AT BOWANNE	PAPTONS BIG TED
		TAPATINA LUCY LOCKETT AT PAPTON
	BOWANNE CRYSTAL GAIL	BOWANNE BOLSHY BERT
		FINNEYHALL RUBY ROSE OF BOWANNE
Dam: BOWANNE BOBBY DAZZLER	BOWANNE BOLSHY BERT	TUSHIELAW CLYDE
		MICHELMAS HOLLY OF BOWANNE
	DODDSLINE DOROTHY AT BOWANNE	DODDSLINE JUST WILLIAM
		DODDSLINE MANDY

Turki 26.1.2002 – 1,1, Best Bitch 2, CC - quality (Championship Show).

Photo by: JOHN HARTLEY PHOTOGRAPHY

BOWANNE MYSTICAL ORCHID UNDER MYSTARZ - JW

Bitch   Born: 9.12.99

Owner: MRS STELLA COOMBES   *Affix: Mystarz*
"MYSTARZ", CHURCH LANE, CLAYDON, IPSWICH, SUFFOLK IP6 0EN
Tel: 01473 831833   E-mail: stella@mystarz.fsnet.co.uk

Breeder: MRS ANNE BOWES

Sire: BOWANNE BRIGHT SPARK	RANWORTH RAMBLER AT BOWANNE	PAPTONS TOP SECRET AT BOWANNE
		BOWANNE CRYSTAL-GAIL
	DODDSLINE JULIANNE AT BOWANNE	BOWANNE BOLSHY BERT
		DODDSLINE SELENA
Dam: BOWANNE BOBBY DAZZLER	BOWANNE BOLSHY BERT	TUSHIELAW CLYDE
		MICHELMAS HOLLY OF BOWANNE
	DODDSLINE DOROTHY	DODDSLINE JUST WILLIAM
		DODDSLINE MANDY

Ebony is the first LH to gain her J.W. since 1997.
This really says it all. (KC Stud Book No. 2050CL).
She also does Obedience and has her Bronze Good Citizen Award.

Photo by: TONY HANCOCK

BOWANNE YULE DELIGHT "Rudy" - Dog Born: 27.12.99

Owners: MR & MRS W.T. & G.M. HANCOCK
9 HIGHFIELD CLOSE, WEST BYFLEET, SURREY KT14 6QR Tel: 01932 400672

Breeder: MRS A.C. BOWES

Sire: CAESAR SUMMER SOLSTICE AT BOWANNE	PAPTONS TOP SECRET AT BOWANNE	PAPTONS BIG BEN
		TAPATINA LUCY LOCKET AT PAPTON
	BOWANNE CRYSTAL GAIL	BOWANNE BOLSHY BERT
		FINNEYHALL RUBY ROSE OF BOWANNE
Dam: BOWANNE BITS'N BOBS	BOWANNE BOLSHY BERT	TUSHIELAW CLYDE
		BOWANNE MICHELMAS HOLLY
	DODDSLINE DOROTHY	DODDSLINE JUST WILLIAM
		DODDSLINE MANDY

28 wins to date: 17 at Championship and 11 at Open Shows, including:

May 01 Crufts .... Judge: Mr Norman Ziman .... 1st Sp. Junior Dog
June 01 Bath .... Judge: Mrs Lynn Bell .... Best Opposite Sex
Aug. 01 W.K.C. .... Judge: Mr Ellis Hulme .... Best Opp. Sex & CC
Sept. 01 Birmingham City ... Judge: Mrs Jane Lilley .... Best of Breed
Oct. 01 L.H. Ch. Show ..... Judge: Miss Kathie Kidd .... Best in Show & CC
Nov. 01 Huntingdonshire ... Judge: Mrs Leana Lewis .... Best of Breed
Dec. 01 L.K.A. .... Judge: Mr Jim Outterside .... Best Opposite Sex
Jan. 02 N.W. & P.B.'s .... Judge: Mrs S. Hewart-Chambers .... B.D. & Reserve B.O.B.
Feb. 02 Cardiff .... Judge: Mrs Atherton/Mr G.Rual .... Best of Breed & Gp 4

Other achievements: The Kennel Club Good Citizen Dog Awards at Bronze, Silver and Gold

Photo by: RUSSELL FINE ARTS

COLNESTAR FEDERAL EXPRESS

Dog   Born: 21.12.93

Owners: JOHN & PAULINE GATER   *Affix: Colnestar*
UPPER HOUSE, CHITTS HILL, COLCHESTER, ESSEX CO3 9SY
Tel: 01206 240100   E-mail: pauline@wgater.fsnet.co.uk

Breeders: P. & J. GATER

Sire: COLNESTAR DYLAN	CHOLLAGEM TOP HAT 'N' TAILS	ROSEADORE BONNIE LADDIE
		CHOLLAGEM MISS MARPLES
	ALICE OF RUDHAM AT COLNESTAR	TEDDY BOY OF TUSHIELAW
		ROSEADORE CURSONS PRIDE
Dam: DODDSLINE DELILAH AT COLNESTAR	DODDSLINE JOE	DODDSLINE BEN (LHC)
		DODDSLINE MANDY
	HAELARBOBS SPINNING JENNY OF DODDSLINE	DODDSLINE BEN (LHC)
		TUSHIELAW BESSIE FROM HAELARBOBS

"Sparky" has been placed at Championship Shows and has been Best of Breed at a number of Open Shows. He qualified for Crufts 2001 and was placed in Veteran.

"Sparky" has also got his Good Citizen Certificate (Obedience).

He is our third generation eye tested clear, and available for stud.

COLNESTAR INKA

Dog   Born: 10.5.98

Owners: JOHN & PAULINE GATER   *Affix: Colnestar*
UPPER HOUSE, CHITTS HILL, COLCHESTER, ESSEX CO3 9SY
Tel: 01206 240100   E-mail: pauline@wgater.fsnet.co.uk

Breeders: P. & J. GATER

Sire: COLNESTAR FEDERAL EXPRESS	COLNESTAR DYLAN	COLLAGEM TOP HAT 'N' TAILS
		ALICE OF RUDHAM AT COLNESTAR
	DODDSLINE DELILAH AT COLNESTAR	DODDSLINE JOE
		HAELARBOBS SPINNING JENNY OF DODDSLINE
Dam: HAELARBOBS BELTANE AT COLNESTAR	HAELARBOBS BARNES WALLIS OF LAUSTEPH	BELLSMOND NAVAJHO
		HAELARBOBS TWO TURTLE DOVES
	HAELARBOBS CASSANDRA	FEATWELLA MAX A MILLION
		STARLOCH SALLY FROM HAELARBOBS

Powerful oversize dog – not into showing,
although has won at Open and Championship Shows, including Crufts.
A very useful gun dog. (Every dog has a purpose).

Photo by: TONY HULL and DAUGHTERS, NORWICH

COLNESTAR JAILHOUSE ROCK AT AUDAXUS   Dog - Born: 14.7.99

Owner: MRS JUDITH SPOONER   *Affix: Audaxus*
CARTREF, 24 WESTFIELD ROAD, TOFTWOOD, DEREHAM, NORFOLK NR19 1JB

Breeders: MR J. & MRS P. GATER

Sire: LANKEELA LISTEN HERE	BOWANNE BOLSHY BERT	TUSHIELAW CLYDE
		MICHELMAS HOLLY OF BOWANNE
	BOWANNE BECKYS GIRL AT LANKEELA	BOWANNE JOLLY ROGER
		FINNEYHALL RUBY ROSE OF BOWANNE
Dam: HAELARBOBS BELTANE AT COLNESTAR	HAELARBOBS BARNES WALLIS	BELLSMOND NAVAJHO
		HAELARBOBS TWO TURTLE DOVES
	HAELARBOBS CASSANDRA	FEATWELLA MAX A MILLION
		STARLOCH SALLY FROM HAELARBOBS

Just a few of Tykes wins:

Birmingham National, April 21st, 2000 - 1st PUPPY DOG, BPIB, judge Mrs E. Lord.
Blackpool Championship Show, June 25th, 2000 - 2nd JUNIOR DOG, judge Mr Harry Baxter.
National & Working Breeds Champ. Show, July 15th, 2000 - 1st JUNIOR DOG, judge Mr A. Wight.
Leeds Championship Show, July 24th, 2000 - 1st JUNIOR DOG, judge Mr Jack Bispham.
Crufts, March 2001 - 1st POST GRADUATE DOG, judge Mr N. Ziman.
Working & Pastoral Breeds Assoc. of Wales, June 16th, 2001 - 1st POSTGRAD. DOG, Mrs J. Collis.
Blackpool Championship Show, June 24th, 2001 - 1st LIMIT DOG, judge Mr L. Lund.

COLNESTAR JIVE TALKING
Bitch   Born: 14.7.99

Owners: JOHN & PAULINE GATER   *Affix: Colnestar*
UPPER HOUSE, CHITTS HILL, COLCHESTER, ESSEX CO3 9SY
Tel: 01206 240100   E-mail: pauline@wgater.fsnet.co.uk

Breeders: P. & J. GATER

Sire: LANKEELA LISTEN HERE	BOWANNE BOLSHY BERT	TUSHIELAW CLYDE
		MICHELMAS HOLLY OF BOWANNE
	BOWANNE BECKYS GIRL AT LANKEELA	BOWANNE JOLLY ROGER
		FINNEYHALL RUBY ROSE OF BOWANNE
Dam: HAELARBOBS BELTANE AT COLNESTAR	HAELARBOBS BARNES WALLIS OF LAUSTEPH	BELLSMOND NAVAJHO
		HAELARBOBS TWO TURTLE DOVES
	HAELARBOBS CASSANDRA	FEATWELLA MAX A MILLION
		STARLOCH SALLY FROM HAELARBOBS

"Libby" has had many wins at both Open and Championship Shows.
Had first litter October 2001.
Sound, friendly bitch, lovely temperament. Typical smiler.
Eye screened Clear – Puppies sometimes available - All puppies eye tested

Photo by: P. GATER

COLNESTAR LIVING DOLL

Bitch   Born: 23.3.01

Owners: JOHN & PAULINE GATER   *Affix: Colnestar*
UPPER HOUSE, CHITTS HILL, COLCHESTER, ESSEX CO3 9SY
Tel: 01206 240100   E-mail: pauline@wgater.fsnet.co.uk

Breeders: P. & J. GATER

Sire: LANKEELA LISTEN HERE	BOWANNE BOLSHY BERT	TUSHIELAW CLYDE
		MICHELMAS HOLLY OF BOWANNE
	BOWANNE BECKYS GIRL AT LANKEELA	BOWANNE JOLLY ROGER
		FINNEYHALL RUBY ROSE OF BOWANNE
Dam: HAELARBOBS BELTANE AT COLNESTAR	HAELARBOBS BARNES WALLIS OF LAUSTEPH	BELLSMOND NAVAJHO
		HAELARBOBS TWO TURTLE DOVES
	HAELARBOBS CASSANDRA	FEATWELLA MAX A MILLION
		STARLOCH SALLY FROM HAELARBOBS

Bex won Minor Puppy at The Lancashire Heeler Club Championship Show at
6 months and a few days, her first time out. Qualified her for Crufts 2002.
Thanks to Miss Kathy Kidd (judge).
This little bitch is totally over exuberant, an absolute bundle of fun.

Photo: PIRKKO TALVITIE

DODDSLINE ELLA

Bitch   Born: 14.3.2000   Reg. No. FIN ER11332701

Owner: MARJATTA LÄHDEKORPI and MARKETTA LÄHDEKORPI
SÖRKÄNTIE 12, 05200 RAJAMÄKI, FINLAND
Tel: 358-40-8321 224   E-mail: marjatta.lahdekorpi@hevosopisto.ypaja.fi

Breeder: N. F. JOHNSTON, GREAT BRITAIN

Sire: DODDSLINE HUMPHRY THE TZAR	DODDSLINE JUST WILLIAM	PIP OF DODDSLINE
		DODDSLINE JESSICA
	DODDSLINE MARCELLA	DODDSLINE CRACER
		DODDSLINE EMILY
Dam: TELPOOLWYN CLARET LADY OF DODDSLINE	TELPOOLWYN ASHRAF	NordV-97 Norduch DKuch THE NIGGARD
		CLASSICAL-CHARM
	DODDSLINE TARA	BLACK DIAMOND OF FINNY
		DODDSLINE MANDY

Nord Winner 2001 – Finnish Winner 2001

Photo: MARKETTA LÄHDEKORPI

DODDSLINE OLGA
Bitch   Born: 23.3.2000   Reg. No. GB AA02701204

Owner: MARKETTA LÄHDEKORPI
JOKIKULMANTIE 111 A, 31700 URJALA AS., FINLAND
Tel: 358-3-546 1143   E-mail: ketta@sci.fi

Breeder: N. F. JOHNSTON, GREAT BRITAIN

Sire: GB. CH. DODDSLINE KRISTEN	GB.CH. DODDSLINE LORD AT SWANNDALE	DODDSLINE BEN
		TAPATINA BE LUCKY OF DODDSLINE
	DODDSLINE LADY SARAH	DODDSLINE JUST WILLIAM
		DODDSLINE TARA
Dam: DODDSLINE ELLIE	DODDSLINE GRACER	BOWANNE BOLSHY BERT
		DODDSLINE SELENA
	DODDSLINE MONICA	DODDSLINE DANNY BOY OF SCARLAC
		DODDSLINE MIRANDA

Photo by: EEVA-MAIJA LEHTINEN

CH. EIJATUUN WELLCOME SANTA - Bitch   Born: 21.12.95

Owner: EEVA-MAIJA LEHTINEN   *Affix: Catellus*
VILNIEMENTIE 3.A.2, 02940 ESPOO, FINLAND
E-mail: eevi@dlc.fi

Breeder: EIJA PELKONEN-LEINO, FINLAND

Sire: W-91, Fin. Ch. ROSEADORE AMBASSADOR ANDY	ACREMEAD SOLO	ACREMEAD MINTO
		ACREMEAD BAMBI
	ACREMEAD BUZZ	ACREMEAD BOGEY
		ACREMEAD GIGI
Dam: RALLARROSENS MILOU	CHOLLAGEM WIFFY-SMIFFY	TUSHIELAW CLYDE
		ROSEADORE CHERRY BLOSSOM
	GISS DINA	TAPATINA NIPPY NOO
		DARLING MARLENE

Marin tulokset: 3 x CC in Finland **FIN CH**
CH. Show Estland, Tallinn, CC, BOB, **EST CH.**
CH. Show Lithuanian, LTU CAC, LTU N, BOB, **LTU CH, LTUW-99**
CH. Show Latvija, Riga, CQ, CAC, BOB, **LA CH.**

Photo by: RUSSELL FINE ARTS

HAELARBOBS BELTANE AT COLNESTAR

Bitch   Born: 7.11.96

Owners: JOHN & PAULINE GATER   *Affix: Colnestar*
UPPER HOUSE, CHITTS HILL, COLCHESTER, ESSEX CO3 9SY
Tel: 01206 240100   E-mail: pauline@wgater.fsnet.co.uk

Breeder: MRS M. OLD

Sire: HAELARBOBS BARNES WALLIS OF LAUSTEPH	BELLSMOND NAVAJHO	HAELARBOBS CLOGGIE ONE-D-BAR AT BELLSMOND
		FOXTHYME BOBBYS GIRL
	HAELARBOBS TWO TURTLE DOVES	LINSEA SINCLAIR LAD
		HAELARBOBS COOSHIE VELVET
Dam: HAELARBOBS CASSANDRA	FEATWELLA MAX A MILLION	DODDSLINE DANDY
		FEATWELLA SWEET DREAMS
	STARLOCH SALLY FROM HAELARBOBS	CHOLLAGEM PAL FOR FOX
		HAELARBOBS GRACIE FIELDS

"Bella" has many wins from Open, Championship, Club Shows and Crufts.
Thanks to Molly Old for letting us have such a nice bitch.
Eye screened clear – Puppies sometimes available - All puppies eye tested.

Photo by: TRACY ST CLAIR PEARCE

HAELARBOBS ULURU TRAQDEAN

Bitch   Born: 10.3.98

Owners: TRACY & PAMELA ST CLAIR PEARCE   *Affix: Traqdean*
SEVEN SAINTS RARE BREEDS, SEVERALLS LANE, COLCHESTER, ESSEX
Tel: 01206 272736   E-mail: sspseven@aol.com

Breeder: MOLLY OLD

Sire: PLAISANCE PETER MERLE OF LAUSTOPH	DODDSLINE MICKEY FINN AT PLAISANCE	DODDSLINE BEN (LHC)
		DODDSLINE TRUDY
	PLAISANCE MISS MERLE	DODDSLINE BEN (LHC)
		EMBAGES RIOTOUS ROSIE
Dam: HAELARBOBS STAR CASCADE	CHOLLAGEM TOP HAT 'N' TAILS	ROSEADORE BONNIE LADDIE
		COLLAGEM MISS MARPLES
	HAELARBOBS COOSHIE VELVET	TUSHIELAW CLYDE
		TUSHIELAW BESSIE FROM HAELARBOBS

A sweet natured girl.

Photo by: E.M. LEHTINEN

LANKEELA FLY BY NIGHT TO KALO

Bitch   Born: 12.3.00

Owner: K.B. KIDD   *Affix: Kalo*
NEWLANDS, 10 PARKWAY, BOGNOR REGIS, SUSSEX PO21 2XR Tel: 01243 863796
Breeder: JACKY CUTLER

		TUSHIELAW CLYDE
Sire: **LANKEELA** **LISTEN HERE**	BOWANNE BOLSHY BERT	MICHAELMASS HOLLY OF BOWANNE
	BOWANNE BECKY'S GIRL AT LANKEELA	BOWANNE JOLLY ROGER
		FINNEYHALL RUBY ROSE OF BOWANNE
Dam: **BOWANNE** **BECKY'S GIRL** **AT LANKEELA**	BOWANNE JOLLY ROGER	TUSHIELAW CLYDE
		MICHAELMASS HOLLY OF BOWANNE
	FINNEYHALL RUBY ROSE OF BOWANNE	BLACK DIAMOND OF FINNEY
		HIGH ENERGY AT REDROSE

BEST A.V.N.S.C. PASTORAL PUPPY - Chichester & D.C.S. Open Show 2001
Qualified for Crufts 2001 and 2002.

Photo by: PAT GORDON

LANKEELA LEGEND HAS IT

Dog   Born: 28.9.97

Owner & Breeder: MISS JACKY CUTLER   *Affix: Lankeela*
76 YEW TREE ROAD, ATTLEBOROUGH, NORFOLK NR17 2RD
Tel: 01953 456893

Sire: TUSHIELAW CLYDE	TEDDY BOY OF TUSHIELAW	TAPATINA MY LAD
		TREASURE OF PENDLESIDE AT TAPATINA
	KENEE JESS	ROSEADORE BONNIE LADDIE
		DORNEY SARA
Dam: BOWANNE BECKY'S GIRL AT LANKEELA	BOWANNE JOLLY ROGER	TUSHIELAW CLYDE
		MICHELMAS HOLLY OF BOWANNE
	FINNEYHALL RUBY ROSE OF BOWANNE	BLACK DIAMOND OF FINNEY
		HIGH ENERGY AT REDROSE

LHC Championship Show - 1st Open Dog (Miss K.B. Kidd)
Driffield Championship Show - 1st Limit Res.B.D. (Mrs S. Cooke)
WKC Championship Show - 1st Limit Dog (Miss Jean Lanning)
(KC Stud Book No. 3385CL)

LAUSTEPH CLANCIE TRAQDEAN

Dog   Born: 26.6.01

Owners: TRACY & PAMELA ST CLAIR PEARCE   *Affix: Traqdean*
SEVEN SAINTS RARE BREEDS, SEVERALLS LANE, COLCHESTER, ESSEX
Tel: 01206 272736   E-mail: sspseven@aol.com

Breeder: LAURA MARTIN

Sire: HAELARBOBS BARNES WALLIS OF LAUSTEPH	BELLSMOND NAVAJHO	HAELARBOBS GLOGGIE ONE-D-BAR OF BELLSMOND
		FOXTHYME BOBBY'S GIRL
	HAELARBOBS TWO TURTLE DOVES	LINSEA SINCLAIR LAD
		HAELARBOBS COOSHIE VELVET
Dam: LAUSTEPH WALTZING MATILDA	PLAISANCE PETER MERLE OF LAUSTEPH	DODDSLINE MICKEY FINN AT PLAISANCE
		PLAISANCE MISS MERLE
	HAELARBOBS MYSTIC MEGAN OF LAUSTEPH	FEATWELLA MAX A MILLION
		STARLOCH SALLY FROM HAELARBOBS

A great temperament, loves everyone.
He enjoyed his first couple of Open Shows with Best Puppy.

Photo by: SUE DOMUN

CH. LEONINE IVY OF RYSLIP - Bitch   Born: 24.9.98

Owner: MRS J. S. CARTLEDGE
71 HORSNEILE LANE, BRACKNELL, BERKS. RG42 2DH   Tel: 01344 641184

Breeder: MRS J. FROGGATT

Sire: CH. DODDSLINE KRISTEN	CH. DODDSLINE LORD AT SWANNDALE	DODDSLINE BEN
		TAPATINA BE LUCKY OF DODDSLINE
	DODDSLINE LADY SARAH	DODDSLINE JUST WILLIAM
		DODDSLINE TARA
Dam: RYSLIP BERTHA	FOXTHYME TOMSK	BOWANNE BOLSHY BERT
		DELSTEPS MADONNA OF FOXTHYME
	DODDSLINE HILDA	BOWANNE BOLSHY BERT
		DODDSLINE TRUDY

CHAMPIONSHIP SHOWS:

Richmond	1999	BPIB
Bournemouth	2000/01	RBOS
WKC	2000	CC & BOB
Richmond	2000	RBOS
LHC (Oct.)	2001	CC & RBIS
B'Ham Nat.	2001	RCC
Blackpool	2001	RCC
SWKA	2001	RBOS
East of England	2001	BOS
WKC	2001	RCC
City of B'Ham	2001	RBOS
LKA	2001	RBOS

OPEN SHOWS:

Coulsdon	2000	BOB
Alton	2000	BAV Pastoral
Maidenhead	2001	BNSC & Pastoral G1
LHC (Feb)	2001	RBIS
LHC (May)	2001	RBIS
Southampton	2001	BOB

And many FIRSTS in AV, NSC and Breed Classes in Junior, P. Grad and Limit.
Gained 3rd. C.C. (and Title) at National Working & Pastoral Breeds Ch. Show 2002.

Photo by: WILLYS PHOTO, Sweden

CH. MONGREL'S FIRST-FIONA - Bitch   Born: 6.5.94

Owner: LENA ELIASSON-SIVERSSON   *Affix: Mongrel's*
PL 4358 SOLLIDEN. 45053 HÄLLEVADSHOLM, SWEDEN
Tel: 0524 504 63   E-mail: karl.p@mail.bip.net

Sire: THE NIGGARD	DODDSLINE BEN	PIP OF DODDSLINE
		CINDY DODDSLINE
	JUDY OF KITT GREEN	BASIL OF MOSSBEACON
		MOTHERS PRIDE
Dam: MONGREL'S CUTIE-CATE	TUSHIELAW DOUGAL AT NALU	ROSEADORE PRINCE SAM-U-EL
		CHOLLAGEM EMY OF TUSHIELAW
	MISS ERMIE OF FINNEYHALL	OSCAR OF BISPHAM
		PIPPA OF BISPHAM

SWEDISH CHAMPION, NORWEGIAN CHAMPION, DANISH CHAMPION,
FINISH CHAMPION, NORDIC WINNER 95-97, KBHW-98, INT. WINNER,
NORWEGIAN WINNER, EUROPEAN WINNER, WORLD WINNER-98,
BEST IN SHOW x 2 at LHC of Sweden – 100 dogs entered

Photo by: CAROL ANN JOHNSON

MONGREL'S UNCLE-UNWIN AT SIMONSVILLE (Imp) Sweden
Dog   Born: 13.6.00

Owner: MR & MRS W. & G. SIMPSON   *Affix: Simonsville*
17 WATER STREET, HAPTON, BURNLEY, LANCS. BB12 7LQ
Tel: 01282 770628   E-mail: Heelers@zoom.co.uk

Breeder: MRS LENA ELIASSON-SIVERSSON

Sire: INT. CH. DODDSLINE KIRK	PATTERJO PLAID	FOXTHYME TOMSK
		DODDSLINE JOY
	DODDSLINE BELLA	DODDSLINE CRACER
		DODDSLINE MIRANDA
Dam: INT. CH. MONGREL'S FIRST-FIONA	INT. CH. THE NIGGARD	DODDSLINE BEN
		JUDY OF KITT GREEN
	SU.CH. MONGREL'S CUTE-CATE	SV-91 SUCH. NUCH. TUSHIELAW DOUGAL AT NALU
		MISS ERMIE OF FINNEYHALL

OPEN SHOWS: 1st x 7   BOB x 1
CHAMP SHOWS: 1st x 4   RBD x 1

Photo: MARKETTA LÄHDEKORPI

MULLE

Dog   Born: 19.11.2000   REG. NO. FIN ER 13754/02

Owner: JUKKA LÄHDEKORPI
JOKIKULMANTIE 111 A, 31700 URJALA AS. FINLAND
Tel: 358-3-546 1143   E-mail: ketta@sci.fi

Breeder: MARJAANA ALAVIUHKOLA, SWEDEN

Sire: SUCH MONGREL'S LAZY-LEROY	SUCH SCAREX GEM'S DONOVAN	SV-91 SUCH NUCH TUSHIELAW DOUGAL AT NALU
		SUCH NUCH WINDER DOUBLE GEM
	NORD.V95, SUCH FINUCH NORDV-97 MONGREL'S FIRST FIONA	NORDV-97 NORDUCH DKUCH THE NIGGARD
		SUCH MONGREL'S CUTIE-CATE
Dam: CISSU	SUCH SCAREX'S GEM'S DONOVAN	SV-91 SUCH NUCH TUSHIELAW DOUGAL AT NALU
		SUCH NUCH WINDER DOUBLE GEM
	MONGREL'S INCREDIBLE-INEZ	NORDV-97 NORDUCH DKUCH THE NIGGARD
		MONGREL'S BLARIE-BLAZE

Finnish Junior Winner 2001, Finnish Winner 2001

SIMONSVILLE RUBY

Bitch   Born: 29.4.01

Owners: MR W. & MRS G. SIMPSON   *Affix: Simonsville*
17 WATER STREET, HAPTON, BURNLEY, LANCS. BB12 7LQ
Tel: 01282 770628   E-mail: Heelers@zoom.co.uk

Breeders: MR W. & MRS G. SIMPSON

Sire: PATTERJO PLAID	FOXTHYME TOMSK	BOWANNE BOLSHY BERT
		DELSTEPS MADONNA OF FOXTHYME
	DODDSLINE JOY	DODDSLINE BEN
		DODDSLINE MANDY
Dam: SIMONSVILLE PEPPER-ANN	CH. DODDSLINE KRISTEN	CH. DODDSLINE LORD AT SWANNDALE
		DODDSLINE LADY SARAH
	BOWANNE LITTLE BROWN JUG	PAPTONS TOP SECRET AT BOWANNE
		DODDSLINE JULIANNE AT BOWANNE

Open Shows:
BOB x 2   BP x 5   GROUP 1 x 1st   1 x 3rd   1 x 4th   8 x 1st

Photo: J. SPOONER

SWANNDALE TINA TURNER AT AUDAXUS

Bitch   Born: 25.9.2000

Owner: MRS JUDITH SPOONER   *Affix: Audaxus*

CARTREF, 24 WESTFIELD ROAD, TOFTWOOD, DEREHAM, NORFOLK NR19 1JB

Breeders: MR & MRS J. SWANN

Sire: CH. DODDSLINE LORD AT SWANNDALE	DODDSLINE BEN (LHC)	PIP OF DODDSLINE
		CINDY DODDSLINE
	TAPATINA BE LUCKY OF DODDSLINE	DODDSLINE BEN (LHC)
		TAPATINA LITTLE GEM
Dam: SWANNDALE BLACK LADY	DARKPRINCE AT SWANNDALE	CH. DODDSLINE LORD AT SWANNDALE
		PATTERJO CANDY
	CHOCOLATE CHIP AT SWANNDALE	CH. DODDSLINE LORD AT SWANNDALE
		PATTERJO HENRIETTA

2001 – the Year of Foot & Mouth – a few of Tina's wins:

Working & Pastoral Breeds Assoc. of Wales Championship Show -
1st PUPPY BITCH, RESERVE BEST OF SEX IN BREED, judge Mrs J. Collis.

Blackpool Championship Show, June 24th, 2001 - 1st PUPPY BITCH, judge Mr L. Lund.

The Welsh Kennel Club Championship Show, August 18th, 2001 -
2nd PUPPY BITCH, judge Mr E. Hulme.

Photo by: TRACY ST CLAIR PEARCE

TRAQDEAN EVIL KIZZMIT
Bitch   Born: 29.9.2000

Owners: TRACY & PAMELA ST CLAIR PEARCE   *Affix: Traqdean*
SEVEN SAINTS RARE BREEDS, SEVERALLS LANE, COLCHESTER, ESSEX
Tel: 01206 272736   E-mail: sspseven@aol.com

Breeders: MISS T. & MRS P. ST. CLAIR PEARCE

Sire: TRAQDEAN DEVIOUS QUEST	PLAISANCE PETER MERLE OF LAUSTEPH	DODDSLINE MICKEY FINN AT PLAISANCE
		PLAISANCE MISS MERLE
	STOURMERE SNAP SHOT WITH TRAQDEAN	BOWANNE BOLSHY BERT
		YEDLIE FELICITE PERPETUE
Dam: TRAQDEAN DEVIOUS QUEENIE	PLAISANCE PETER MERLE OF LAUSTEPH	DODDSLINE MICKEY FINN AT PLAISANCE
		PLAISANCE MISS MERLE
	STOURMERE SNAP SHOT WITH TRAQDEAN	BOWANNE BOLSHY BERT
		YEDLIE FELICITE PERPETUE

A born ratter and bunny hunter.

TRAQDEAN JAUNTY NIQUITA
Bitch   Born: 25.1.99

Owners: TRACY & PAMELA ST CLAIR PEARCE   *Affix: Traqdean*
SEVEN SAINTS RARE BREEDS, SEVERALLS LANE, COLCHESTER, ESSEX
Tel: 01206 272736   E-mail: sspseven@aol.com

Breeders: MISS T. & MRS P. ST. CLAIR PEARCE

Sire: TRAQDEAN DEVIOUS QUEST	PLAISANCE PETER MERLE OF LAUSTEPH	DODDSLINE MICKEY FINN AT PLAISANCE
		PLAISANCE MISS MERLE
	STOURMERE SNAP SHOT WITH TRAQDEAN	BOWANNE BOLSHY BERT
		YEDLIE FELICITE PERPETUE
Dam: HAELARBOBS HARVEST SUPPER WITH TRAQDEAN	BELLSMOND CHEROKEE	DODDSLINE KENTEE JAKE
		BELLSMOND SHOSHONEE
	STARLOCH SALLY FROM HAELARBOBS	CHOLLAGEM PAL FOR FOX
		HAELARBOBS GRACIE FIELDS

Our expert bunny hunter.

TUSHIELAW CLYDE – Dog Born: 3.8.85

Owner: MISS SARAH A. WHYBROW   *Affix: Sarcasha*
VIRGINIA HOUSE, FOXLEY, EAST DEREHAM, NORFOLK

Breeder: MRS D.C. CARGEN

Sire: TEDDY BOY OF TUSHIELAW	TAPATINA MY LAD	LADDIE OF PENDLESIDE AT TAPATINA
		FENISCOWLES PRINCESS TESSY
	TREASURE OF PENDLESIDE AT TAPATINA	TICH
		PIP
Dam: KENEE JESS	ROSEADORE BONNIE LADDIE	FENISCOWLES EARL BUMBLEBEE
		ACREMEAD BUZZ
	SARA OF DORNEY	ACREMEAD BOGEY
		FENISCOWLES PRINCESS SUZY

BEST OF BREED, Crufts 1989, 1990, 1991, 1993, 1994, 1995 (6 times).
Over 50 BOBs at Championship Shows.
Top LH "Our Dogs"/Omega Rare Breed Contest 1994
Representative for the Breed at Contest of Champions (London) 1994.

ADVERTISEMENT SECTION

EAST of ENGLAND LANCASHIRE HEELER CLUB

(proposed)

founded 1996

Chairperson
Jacky Cutler
Tel: 01953 456893

Secretary
Sarah Whybrow
Tel: 01362 688734

Treasurer/Memberships
Stella Coombes
"Mystarz", Church Lane, Claydon,
Ipswich, Suffolk IP6 0EN
Tel: 01473 831833

For impartial help and advice on all aspects of
Lancashire Heelers please contact any of the above.

Various events held throughout the year.

PENNIJAR PILGRIM

March 4, 2000
Sire: Dark Prince at Swanndale   Dam: Pennijar Baby Spice
Breeder: Joan and Mark Smith
PENNIJAR LANCASHIRE HEELERS

Pennijar Pilgrim, "Hoover"
The First Lancashire Heeler
to be accepted to
The American Kennel Club
Foundation Stock Service Registry

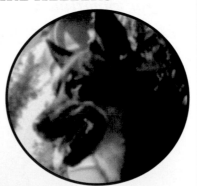

Lancashire Heelers, USA
www.lancashireheelersusa.com
e-mail: jayne@lancashireheelersusa.com

"MYSTARZ"

Lancashire Heelers and Swedish Vallhunds
Ebony   Kia   Calli

Photo taken by STELLA COOMBES

The home of the Happy Heelers and friends
Bowanne Mystical Orchid Under Mystarz - JW
Bowanne Miss Molly Under Mystarz
& Starvon East Rose Under Mystarz
Ebony, the first Lancashire Heeler to gain a
Junior Warrant since 1997 (see Portrait Gallery)
All adults and puppies eye tested.

A small, select breeder where health, quality and
sound temperaments are of paramount importance.
Carefully bred puppies of both breeds sometimes available to approved homes.

Proudly owned, loved and shown by STELLA COOMBES
"Mystarz", Church Lane, Claydon, Ipswich, Suffolk IP6 0EN
Tel: 01473 831833 — Enquiries welcome

SWANNDALE LANCASHIRE HEELERS

CH. DODDSLINE LORD AT SWANNDALE
"Sam" to his friends

Sire: Doddsline Ben
Dam: Tapatina Be Lucky of Doddsline

Photo by: JOHN HARTLEY

Lord was Top Heeler 1995-96-97, Top Male 1998-99-2000-2001.
Best Dog at Crufts three times and lots more.

"Sam" is now almost 10 and is in semi retirement.
At his last club show on the 24th February, 2002, judge Mrs G. Simpson,
he won Best Veteran, Best Dog and Res. Best in Show.

We would like to congratulate Lords children and grandchildren
on their many wins . . .

FINNISH CH. ATOMOUI KYISHA	SWANNDALE BLACK LADY
ENGLISH CH. DODDSLINE KRISTEN	SWANNDALE BLACK IRIS
SWANNDALE BLACK ORCHID	DARK PRINCE AT SWANNDALE
SWANNDALE THE BLACKSMITH AT SALROYD	BLACK KNIGHT AT SWANNDALE
SWANNDALE BLACK DIAMOND	NORMANSVILLE IDAHO
SWANNDALE BLACK BARON	LUCKY LOCKET
SWANNDALE BLACK ROSE	DODDSLINE SONNY AT SIMONS VILLE
SWANNDALE BLACK PRINCE	ATOMOHI JOHNNY COME LATELEY
SWANNDALE BLACK PRINCESS	ATOMOHI KEYHOLE KATE
SWANNDALE BLACK ADDER AT KORMAC	DODDSLINE TILLY MINT AT SWANNDALE

And many many more – well done on your wins.

SWANNDALE LANCASHIRE HEELERS

Photo of SWANNDALE FRANK BRUNO, who now lives in Finland
with Anna Muerman. As you can see he is a nice liver and tan dog.
He is now doing Agility and loves it.

His sister SWANNDALE TINA TURNER AT AUDAXUS,
owned by Judy Spooner in England is doing well in the ring
and took second at Crufts in her class, she is also a liver and tan.

by: Ch. Doddsline Lord at Swanndale ex: Swanndale Black Lady

All Swanndale Heelers are eye tested and clear of CEA.
Dogs at stud to selected bitches – Puppies sometimes available.

Enquires to: **MR JOHN & JULIA SWANN "SWANNDALE KENNELS"**
480 CRANKWOOD ROAD, LEIGH, LANCASHIRE, ENGLAND WN7 4PP
Tel: 01942 676545 Mobile: 07971351242 E-mail: julia~@swanndale.fsnet.co.uk

ANIMALCOMPANIET

Mog-Ur's Fru Betty

Born: 3.3.97

BLACK & TAN

BREEDER: EVA BRAUER

Sire:
Ringhells
Uncas the Heeler

Dam:
Mongrel's
Gleamy-Glenda

Photo by: MAUD LINDQVIST

KENNEL

ANIMALCOMPANIET

LANCASHIRE
HEELER

Maud Lindqvist, Byvägen 43, 816 31 Ockelbo, SWEDEN
+46 – (0)297 60055
E-mail: maudlindqvist@hotmail.com
http://home.swipnet.se/animalcompaniet
(english text under construction)

ANIMALCOMPANIET

Mog-Ur's Fru Elli

Born: 20.5.98

LIVER & TAN

BREEDER: EVA BRAUER

Sire:
Stardogs Sicke'n'En

Dam:
Ringhells Venus

Photo by: MAUD LINDQVIST

Photo by: MAUD LINDQVIST

Animal-companiets Alva-Cowgirl

Born: 16.11.99

LIVER & TAN

BREEDER: MAUD LINDQVIST

Sire:
Stardogs Sicke'n'En

Dam:
Mog-Ur's Fru Betty

107

Heelers from Finland

From left to right: **Bowanne Lollypop Lil** - born: 16.2.01
(Caesar Summer Solstice at Bowanne – Bowanne Bobby Dazzler)
BREEDER: ANNE BOWES, ENGLAND. OWNER: LILIAN HAKKARAINEN.

FIN CH, W-2000 Stardogs Va' Du' Vill - born: 8.7.95
(Scarex Jon-Jon Charming Dog – Embages Rushon Rita)
BREEDER: IRENE BÖRLIN, SWEDEN. OWNER: LILIAN HAKKARAINEN.

**FIN&EST&LTU&LA CH, LTU W-99
Eijatuun Wellcome Santa** - born: 21.12.95
(Ch. Roseadore Ambassador Andy – Rallarrosens Milou)
BREEDER: EIJA PELKONEN-LEINO, FINLAND. OWNER: EEVA-MAIJA LEHTINEN.

Lilian Hakkarainen
Rahapajankatu 1 C 11
00160 Helsinki, Finland
Phone: +358 9 611575

Eeva-Maija Lehtinen
Vilniementie 3 A 2
02940 Espoo, Finland.
Phone: +358 9 595476
e-mail: eevi@dlc.fi

Atomohi LANCASHIRE HEELERS

Photo by: JOY SMITH

ATOMOHI JOHNNY COME LATELEY - DOB: 8/9/99
Sire: CH. Doddsline Lord at Swanndale
Dam: Swanndale Black Pearl at Atomohi
CEA Clear at 7 weeks
Litter brother to Finnish Champion Atomohi Khyisa

We also have ... DODDSLINE RUSTY AT ATOMOHI - CEA Clear
SWANNDALE BLACK PEARL AT ATOMOHI - CEA Clear

Both dogs are offered at stud to approved bitches.

David and Joy Smith
ATOMOHI LODGE, BIDWELL HILL, HOUGHTON REGIS,
DUNSTABLE, BEDS. LU5 5DR   Tel: 01582 862685

COLNESTAR

"DYLAN"
The Late COLNESTAR DYLAN
BORN 20/06/1989 TO 18/02/2000
SIRE: CHOLLAGEM TOP HAT 'N' TAILS
DAM: ALICE OF RUDHAM AT COLNESTAR
HE QUALIFIED FOR CRUFTS 1990/91/92/93/94/95/96/98/99/2000/01
Best Veteran in Breed at Crufts 1999

A wonderful show dog, many many wins and was always the dog to use for demonstrations at Obedience Classes. Dylan loved to please, as many junior handlers know. He was used in competition by a number of junior handlers, and took one of them to The Richmond Finals, they did not win unfortunately.

His line has been the foundation of our breeding.

FURTHER INFORMATION FROM: **JOHN** and **PAULINE GATER**
UPPER HOUSE, CHITTS HILL, COLCHESTER, ESSEX CO3 9SY
TEL: 01206 240100/240187 E-MAIL PAULINE@WGATER.FSNET.CO.UK

COLNESTAR LANCASHIRE HEELERS
BEX AND SPARKY

PHOTO BY PAULINE GATER

COLNESTAR LIVING DOLL AND COLNESTAR FEDERAL EXPRESS

Bex qualified for Crufts first time out at The Lancashire Heeler Club Championship Show. Sparky has had many wins including Crufts. To us, like most small breeders, quality is more essential than quantity, as is temperament.

All litters are home reared.

All breeding stock eye tested clear - Puppies sometimes available.

See Portrait Gallery for Pedigrees

DOGS AT STUD

FURTHER INFORMATION FROM: **JOHN** and **PAULINE GATER**
UPPER HOUSE, CHITTS HILL, COLCHESTER, ESSEX CO3 9SY
TEL: 01206 240100/240187
E-MAIL PAULINE@WGATER.FSNET.CO.UK
PAULINE@COLNESTAR.FSNET.CO.UK

SOME OF THE EARLY
LANCASHIRE HEELER SHOW RESULTS
(Before the dog or the Club were K.C. recognised)

Just some of the known Show Results are given in this book. Space restricts the inclusion of all the known results. It will be noticed that some of the early dogs were referred to by pet names only. Many did not have Affixes. Where known, the owners name appears too.

Brooke, Norwich, July 1st, 1978
Judge: Mr Ben Johnson

Best in Show	"Mac"	Mrs Osborne, Hants
Res. Best in Show	"Bracken"	Mrs Welch, Norfolk
Best Puppy	"Tansey"	Mrs Welch, Norfolk
Best Veteran	"Noddy"	Mrs Illingworth, Lancashire

North Walsham, Norfolk, July 24th, 1978
Judge: Mr J. Todrayner

Best in Show	"Tansey	Mrs Welch, Norfolk
Best Dog	"Sam"	Mrs Relva, Norfolk
Best Bitch	"Tansey"	Mrs Welch, Norfolk
Best Puppy	"Tansey"	Mrs Welch, Norfolk
Best Veteran	"Sam"	Mrs Relva, Norfolk

Ripponden Open Meeting, Yorkshire, Sept. 23rd, 1978
Judge: Mr J. Moore

Best in Show	"Noddy"	Mrs Illingworth, Lancashire
Res. Best in Show	"Twiggy"	Miss Pritt, Norfolk
Best Bitch	"Twiggy"	Miss Pritt, Norfolk
Best Dog	"Noddy"	Mrs Illingworth, Lancashire
Best Puppy	"Tessa"	Mrs P. Taylor, Clitheroe, Lancs.
Best Veteran	"Noddy"	Mrs Illingworth, Lancashire

Yorks, Black House Farm, April 26th, 1979

Puppy Class 1	Berghof Sally (Best Yorkshire Exhibit)	
Dog Class 2	Acremead Yorkshire Boy (Max)	
Best Veteran	Sammy (Res. Best in Show)	
2nd Puppy Class	Tiny	
2nd Novelty Class	Berghof Beauty	
Best in Show & Best Bitch	Bracken	Mrs Pam Welch

North Walsham Football Ground, June 3rd, 1979

Judge: Kate Muirhead

CLASS RESULTS

(Note: not all Full Results are known for some of these Shows. Also the Classification varied. But it is very interesting to see which dog won classes and who was there at the time).

CLASS 1 – PUPPY

1. Greenridges Michelmas	R. Wagner
2. Feniscowles Earl Bumblebee	Mrs Rush
3. Acremead Googie	Mrs Mackintosh

CLASS 2 – DOG OPEN

1. Greenridges Michelmas	R. Wagner
2. Cornwallis Paddington Bear	Dr Macleod
3. Feniscowles Earl Bumblebee	Mrs Rush

16th May, 1979, Lancashire (Spring Meeting)

CLASS 1 – PUPPY

1. Berghof Sally	Mrs Greenwood, Yorkshire
2. Tiny	Mrs Welsh, Lancashire
3. Feniscowles Princess Cleo	Mrs Gilman, Lancashire

CLASS 2 – DOG

1. Cornwallis Paddington Bear	Dr MacLeod, Norfolk
2. Acremead Yorkshire Boy	Miss Kemp, Yorkshire
3. Acremead Misto	Mrs Johnson, Shropshire

CLASS 3 – BITCH

1. Acremead Gay	Mrs Welch, Norfolk
2. Acremead Minnie	Miss Pritt, Norfolk
3. Shandy	Mrs Laraway, Lancashire

CLASS 4 – VETERAN

1. Sammy	Mrs Walsh, Lancashire
2. Acremead Pippa	Miss Jude, Norfolk
3. Sally	Mrs Lowe, Shropshire

Rackheath, Norwich, Norfolk
Judge: F.G. Bristow

CLASS 1 – PUPPY DOG
1. Berghof Lustig   Mrs Webster
2. Greenridges Michelmas   Mr R. Wagner
3. Feniscowles Prinz   Mrs Gilman

CLASS 2 – PUPPY BITCH
1. Pendleside Treasure   Mrs Taylor
2. Princess Susan   Mrs Aldrich
3. Greenridges Bramble   Mrs Brighty
4. Pendleside Lady Penelope   Mrs Taylor
5. Greenridges Bryony   Mrs Welch

CLASS 3 – NOVICE D/B
1. Pendleside Treasure   Mrs Taylor
2. Berghof Lustig   Mrs Webster
3. Princess Susan   Mrs Aldrich
4. Ben   Mrs Chapman
5. Greenridges Bryony   Mrs Welch

CLASS 4 – OPEN DOG
1. Cornwallis Paddington Bear   Dr MacLeod, Norfolk
2. Greenridges Michelmas   Mr R. Wagner
3. Ben   Mrs Chapman
4. Feniscowles King Shany   Mrs Gilman
5. Bill   Mrs Chapman

CLASS 5 – OPEN BITCH
1. Acremead Tiggy   Miss Pritt
2. Berghof Sally   Mrs Greenwood
3. Cornwallis Rachel   Miss Church
4. Pendleside Treasure   Mrs Taylor
5. Acremead Gay (Bracken)   Mrs Welch

CLASS 6 – VETERAN
1. Sally   Mrs Lowe
2. Acremead Bogey   Mrs Mackintosh
3. KoKo   Mrs Unwin
4. Acremead Pippa   Miss Jude
5. Acremead Busy Bee   Mrs Welch

CLASS 7 – CHILD HANDLING

1.	Berghof Tansey	R. Wagner
2.	Honey Bee	
3.	Mr Bumble	Mrs Rush
4.	Pendleside Lady Penelope	Mrs Taylor
5.	Greenridges Bramble	Mrs Brighty

CLASS 8 – CONSOLATION

1.	Sadie	Mrs Lowe
2.	Googie	Mrs Mackintosh
3.	Berghof Tansey	R. Wagner
4.	Mr Bumble	Mrs Rush
5.	Acremead Boy Mac	Mrs Osborn

BEST IN SHOW	Berghof Lustig
Res. Best in Show	Acremead Tiggy
Best. Yorks.	Berghof Lustig

Quite a number of the early exhibitors did not have Affixes so the dogs just had one (pet) name. However, the affix of "Acremead" (belonging to Mrs Mackintosh) set the example for others. (In fact Mrs Mackintosh had two affixes, the other being Macbrook, under which she showed her other dogs). Among the early Lancashire Heeler Affixes are a few listed below, and to whom they belonged.

Acremead	Mrs G. Mackintosh	(Norfolk)
Berghof	Mrs M. Webster	(Norfolk & Yorkshire)
Cornwallis	Miss A. Pritt	(Norfolk)
Dorney	Mrs D. Aldrich	(Norfolk)
Feniscowles	Mrs A. Gilman	(Lancashire)
Greenridges	Mrs P. Welch	(Norfolk)
Roseadore	Mrs D. Rush	(Norfolk)
Settena	Mrs Leech	(Lancashire)

This was
"BERGHOF TANSEY"

owned by
Mrs P. Welch

(bred by
Mrs M. Webster).

Born: 19.9.1977.

Sire:
Sam (unregistered)

Dam:
Berghof Beauty.

This is a good photo
showing the tail curved
over back when alerted.
Also shows erect ears.

<small>Photo by permission of</small>
<small>Mrs P. Welch</small>

<small>Photo by E.M. LEHTINEN</small>

This was "BERGHOF KATE" owned by Mrs D. Rush (bred by Mrs M. Webster).
Born: 23.10.1980 This is a good photo taken over 22 years ago showing conformation and plenty
of daylight under body (which is very important if the heeler is to keep its agility in the future)

RESULTS OF THE LANCASHIRE HEELER CLUB SHOWS

Held under Kennel Club Rules – The Early Years up to 1989

Before 1984, the Lancashire Heeler Club held its own shows, but these were not under Kennel Club Rules, (as the Club was not registered). Prior to this, some results are recorded but space does not permit them all to be included here. Results here are up to 1989, **before** the Lancashire Heeler Club produced Handbooks. Current Show News can be obtained from Club Secretary).

THE FIRST LANCASHIRE HEELER CLUB MEMBERS' LIMITED SHOW held on SATURDAY, 19th MAY, 1984

At Rackheath Village Hall, Rackheath, near Norwich, Norfolk.

Judge was Miss Ferelith Hamilton (All Rounder)

38 Dogs were entered, making 104 entries.

		Owned by:	*Bred by:*
Best in Show:	Roseadore Black Beauty of Chesara	Mrs J. Kirk	Mrs A. Greenall
Res. B.I.S.:	Acremead Buzz	Mrs D. Rush	Mrs G. Mackintosh
Best Opp. Sex:	Acremead Buzz	Mrs D. Rush	Mrs G. Mackintosh
Best Puppy:	Roseadore Prince Samuel	Mrs D. Rush	Br. Exhibitor

THE FIRST LANCASHIRE HEELER OPEN SHOW held on SATURDAY, 6th OCTOBER, 1984

At Samlesbury Memorial Hall, Samlesbury, near Preston, Lancashire.

Judge was Mr Jack Bennet

35 Dogs were entered, making 88 entries.

Best in Show:	Chainy	Mrs A. Stringfellow
Res. B.I.S.:	Tapatina My Lad	Mrs P. Taylor
Best Puppy:	High Energy at Redrose	Mr G. Stephenson & Mr H. Marsh

THE SECOND MEMBERS LIMIT LANCASHIRE HEELER CLUB SHOW held on SATURDAY, 18th MAY, 1985

At Rackheath Village Hall, Rackheath, near Norwich, Norfolk.

Judge was Mr David Cavill

47 Dogs were entered, making 138 entries.

Best in Show:	Roseadore Cherry Blossom	Mr & Mrs Belson
Res. B.I.S. &		Mrs D. Rush
Best Opp. Sex:	Roseadore Bonnie Laddie	Mrs & Miss Brown
Best Puppy:	Donreithe Double Dealer	Mrs S. Taylor
		Mrs D. Rush
		Mrs M. Sharples

THE THIRD LANCASHIRE HEELER CLUB MEMBERS LIMIT SHOW held on 5th OCTOBER, 1985

At Samlesbury Memorial Hall, Samlesbury, near Preston, Lancashire.

Judge was Mr R. Goodson

45 Dogs were entered, making 138 entries.

Best in Show:	Pepi of Winder	Mr & Mrs Morphet
Res. B.I.S.: &		Mrs Thompson
Best Opp. Sex:	Broadfield Chainy	Mrs A. Stringfellow
Best Puppy:	The Tramp of the Embages	Miss D. E. Malins
		Mrs Greenall
		Mrs Morphet

THE FOURTH LANCASHIRE HEELER CLUB MEMBERS LIMIT SHOW held on 17th MAY, 1986

At Rackheath Village Hall, Rackheath, near Norwich, Norfolk.

Judge was Mr Jack Peachey

46 Dogs were entered, making 110 entries.

Best in Show:	High Energy at Redrose	Mr & Mrs Higham
Res. B.I.S.: &		Mr Johnston
Best Opp. Sex:	Donreithe Double Dealer	Mrs S. Taylor
Best Puppy:	Tushielaw Clyde	Miss S. Whybrow
		Mrs M. Sharples
		Mrs D. Cargen

THE FIFTH LANCASHIRE HEELER CLUBS MEMBERS LIMIT SHOW held on SATURDAY, 4th OCTOBER, 1986

At Samlesbury Memorial Hall, Samlesbury, near Preston, Lancashire.

Judge was Mr Graham Newell

45 Dogs were entered, making 122 entries.

Best in Show:	Black Diamond of Finneyhall	Mr & Mrs Higham
Res. B.I.S.:	Pip of Doddsline	Mr N. Johnston
Best Opp. Sex:	Acremead Biscuit of Kalo	Mrs & Miss Kidd
Best Puppy:	Risehill Susie of Finneyhall	Mr & Mrs Higham

Mr N. Johnston
Mr Fisher
Mrs G. Mackintosh
Miss S. Tickle

THE SIXTH LANCASHIRE HEELER CLUBS MEMBERS LIMIT SHOW held on SATURDAY, 16th MAY, 1987

At Rackheath Village Hall, Rackheath, near Norwich, Norfolk.

Judge was Mrs Pamela Cross Stern

45 Dogs were entered, making 112 entries.

Best in Show:	Tushielaw Clyde	Miss S. Whybrow
Res. B.I.S. &		
Best Opp. Sex:	Risehill Sadie of Finneyhall	Mr & Mrs Higham
Best Puppy:	Finneyhall Tarragon of Sandpits	Mrs W. Lewis

Mrs D. Cargen

Miss Tickle
Mr Higham

THE SEVENTH LANCASHIRE HEELER CLUBS MEMBERS LIMIT SHOW held on SATURDAY, 3rd OCTOBER, 1987

At Samlesbury Memorial Hall, near Preston, Lancashire.

Judge was Mrs Ann Davis (Loakespark)

63 Dogs were entered, making 136 entries.

Best in Show:	Merry Meg of the Embages	Miss D. Malins
Res. B.I.S.:	Pepi of Winder	Mr & Mrs Morphet
Best Opp. Sex:	The Tramp of the Embages	Miss D. Malins
Best Puppy:	Foxthyme Hidden Treasure	Mrs E. Lord

Mr Hicks
Mrs Thompson
Mrs Morphet
Br. Exhibitor

THE EIGHTH LANCASHIRE HEELER CLUBS MEMBERS LIMIT SHOW held on SATURDAY, 23rd APRIL, 1988
At Rackheath Village Hall, Rackheath, near Norwich, Norfolk.

Judge was Mrs M. Webster (Berghof)
60 Dogs were entered, making 127 entries.

Best in Show: Res. B.I.S.: &	Finneyhall Tarragon of Sandpits	Mr Higham
Best Opp. Sex:	Acremead Biscuit of Kalo	Mrs G. Mackintosh
Best Puppy:	Chollagem Wiffy Smiffy	Br. Exhibitor

THE NINTH LANCASHIRE HEELER CLUBS MEMBERS LIMIT SHOW held on SATURDAY, 1st OCTOBER, 1988
At Samlesbury Memorial Hall, near Preston, Lancashire.

Judge was Dr Ben Raven
76 Dogs were entered, making 146 entries.

Best in Show: Res. B.I.S.: &	Black Diamond of Finneyhall	Mr Johnston
Best Opp. Sex:	Tapatina Toyah's Dream	Br. Exhibitor
Best Puppy:	Mouse of Mytchett	Mrs Vincent

THE TENTH LANCASHIRE HEELER CLUBS MEMBERS LIMIT SHOW held on SATURDAY, 13th MAY, 1989
At North Walsham Community Centre, North Walsham, Norfolk.

Judge was Mr M. Stockman, M.R.C.V.S.
48 Dogs were entered, making 100 entries.

Best in Show:	Bowanne Bolshy Bert	Br. Exhibitor
Res. B.I.S.:	Rocky of Kitt Green	Br. Exhibitor
Best Opp. Sex:	Doddsline Mandy	Br. Exhibitor
Best Puppy:	Chollagem Hope'n Glory	Mr & Mrs Belson

THE FIRST CHAMPIONSHIP SHOW TO PUT ON LANCASHIRE HEELER CLASSES

The first Championship Show to put on Lancashire Heeler Classes was Blackpool (without Challenge Certificates, of course). This was in 1982 (the breed was only Kennel Club recognised in 1981). The judge was (the late) Mr Ben Johnson (the man who helped to formulate the Lancashire Heeler Breed Standard). There were ten classes with five exhibitors entered and eight Lancashire Heelers entered (but Mrs Mackintosh and her bitch Acremead Googie were absent on the day). This left four exhibitors with seven dogs there. This meant in four classes there was only one dog entered. Another four classes only had two dogs entered (which with an absentee meant that a dog stood alone in a further two classes). The two largest classes had three dogs entered (but minus absentees) meant only two dogs competing. On this historic occasion, it poured with rain and the Lancashire Heelers were judged outside. It rained so much, the water was running off the Trilby hat that Ben Johnson was wearing! For these Classes the Brewing firm of Whitbread's had kindly given a shield named after them. (The Secretary of the Blackpool Championship Show at the time was Mr Jack Bennett).

THE WHITBREAD SHIELD HAS BEEN WON BY THE FOLLOWING BEST OF BREED WINNERS

(The Early Years up to 1988)

1982

Judge was Mr Ben Johnson

8 Dogs were entered, making 18 entries.

		Owned by:	*Bred by:*
B.O.B.:	Tamara of Tapatina NAF (B) (Feniscowles Princess Tessie)	Mrs P. Taylor	Mrs A. Gilman
R.B.O.B.:	Roseadore Black Beauty	Mrs J. Kirk	Mrs D. Rush
R.B.D.:	Crackybobs at Broomishaw and Chesara	Mrs J. Elsden	Mr Prescott
B.P.:	Roseadore Black Beauty		

1983

Judge was Mr H. Baxter

18 Dogs were entered, making 48 entries.

B.O.B.:	Tapatina Little Gem (B)	Mrs P. Taylor	Br. Exhibitor
R.B.O.B.:	Tapatina My Lad	Mrs P. Taylor	Br. Exhibitor
R.B.D.:	Teddy Boy of Tushielaw	Mrs D. Cargen	Mrs P. Taylor
R.B.B.:	Acremead Biscuit	Mrs & Miss Kidd	Mrs G. Mackintosh
B.P.:	Tapatina Little Gem		

1984

Judge was Mrs V. Yates

36 Dogs were entered, making 60 entries.

B.O.B.:	Redrose Polly Flinders (B)	Mr G. Stephenson & Mr H. Marsh	Mr Cable-Alexander
R.B.O.B.:	Tapatina My Lad	Mrs P. Taylor	Br. Exhibitor
R.B.D.:	Roseadore Black Beauty of Chesara		
R.B.B.:	Chesara Heela Ivy	Miss S. Bilborough	Mrs Elsden
B.P.:	Redrose Polly Flinders		

1985

Judge was Miss K. Kidd

35 Dogs were entered, making 75 entries.

B.O.B.:	Roseadore Black Beauty of Chesara (D)		
R.B.O.B.:	Sandpits Earthsmoke	Mrs W.T. Lewis	Br. Exhibitor
R.B.B.:	Pepi of Winder	Mr & Mrs Morphet	Mrs Thompson
R.B.D.:	Pip of Doddsline	Mr N. Johnston	Mr F. Fisher
B.P.:	Sandpits Earthsmoke		

122

1986

Judge was Mr L. Lund
36 Dogs were entered, making 63 entries.

B.O.B.:	Black Diamond of Finney (D)	Mr & Mrs W. Higham	Mr N. Johnston
R.B.O.B.:	Sandpits Earthsmoke		Mr W. Higham
R.B.B.:	Kenive Rose	Miss D. Malins	
R.B.D.:	Roseadore Black Beauty of Chesara		
B.P.:	Risehill Trixie	Miss S. Tickle	Br. Exhibitor

1987

Judge was Mr H. A. Jordan
36 Dogs were entered, making 69 entries.

B.O.B.:	Acremead Biscuit of Kalo (B)	Mrs & Miss Kidd	Mrs G. Mackintosh
R.B.O.B.:	Black Diamond of Finney Hall		
R.B.D.:	Tapatina My Lad		
R.B.B.:	Kenelaine Gem	Mr & Mrs K. Moore	Mr & Mrs Higham
B.P.:	Emanday Golden Gloves	Mrs P. Taylor	Mrs Genovese

1988

Judge was Mr E. Hulme
42 Dogs were entered, making 72 entries.

B.O.B.:	Tushielaw Clyde (D)	Miss S. Whybrow	Mrs D. Cargen
R.B.O.B.:	Acremead Biscuit of Kalo		
R.B.B.:	Kenelaine Gem		
R.B.D.:	Black Diamond of Finney		
B.P.:	Finneyhall Emerald Lady at Maydon	Mrs M. Gordon	Mr Higham

123

JUNIOR WARRANT (Updated to 2001)

The first Lancashire Heeler to gain a Junior Warrant was BLACK DIAMOND OF FINNEY (D). He was owned by Mr & Mrs W. Higham and bred by Mr N. Johnston. News of this appeared in the March 1987 Newsletter. This was under the old system when qualification was 25 points gained when a puppy was from 6-18 months old.

IN 1995   *(old system)* PATTERJO POLKA AT PENNIJAR gained a Junior Warrant. (Owned by Mr & Mrs M. Smith and bred by Mrs J. Patrick)

IN 1997   *(old system)* PENNIJAR TALK OF THE NORTH won a Junior Warrant. (Owned and bred by Mr & Mrs M. Smith).

IN 1997   *(old system)* DODDSLINE DUKE won a Junior Warrant. (Owned by Dr & Mrs Jack Hopper and bred by Mr N. Johnston.)

2001   Saw the first Junior Warrant Winner gaining the title under the *New System*, being entered in Kennel Club Stud Book. This was a bitch, BOWANNE MYSTICAL ORCHID UNDER MYSTARZ (Stud Book No. 2050CL). Owned by Mrs S. Coombes and bred by Mrs A. Bowes).

CUPS AND TROPHIES OF THE LANCASHIRE HEELER CLUB (as at 1989)

Norfolk Lancashire Heeler Club Shows have the following:

BEST IN SHOW:	MACKINTOSH CHALLENGE TROPHY	Given by Mrs G. Mackintosh
RESERVE BEST IN SHOW:	THE MACKINTOSH TROPHY	Given by Mrs G. Mackintosh
BEST OPPOSITE SEX:		
BEST PUPPY IN SHOW:	SANDPITS CUP	Given by Mr & Mrs M. Lewis
BEST PUPPY BITCH:	HAELARBOBS CUP	Given by Mrs M. Old

BEST JUNIOR:	TUSHIELAW CUP	Given by Mrs D. Cargen
BEST NOVICE:	MANX TROPHY	Given by Mrs G. Skinner
OPEN BITCH:	CATELLUS VASE	Given by Miss E. Lehtinen (Finland)
SPECIAL ELIMINATOR:	KALO AWARD	Given by Miss K. Kidd
BEST NORFOLK LANCASHIRE HEELER		
BEST LANCASHIRE LANCASHIRE HEELER		
BEST YORKSHIRE LANCASHIRE HEELER		
BEST "OTHER COUNTIES" LANCASHIRE HEELER		

Note: THE MACKINTOSH TROPHY for RESERVE BEST IN SHOW was presented in 1988 by Mrs Mackintosh at the Norfolk Lancashire Heeler Club Show (which was also the 10th Anniversary of the Club formatting the standard). It was her wish that this Trophy (which is a silver tankard) should be held between Norfolk and Lancashire alternatively, which means the winner holds it approx. 6 months. It is at each show for Reserve Best in Show.

Lancashire based Lancashire Heeler Club Shows have the following: (as at 1989)

BEST IN SHOW:	THE ELIZABETH MOORE TROPHY	Given by Mr & Mrs K. Moore
RESERVE BEST IN SHOW:	THE FOXTHYME TROPHY	Given by Mrs E. Lord
RESERVE BEST IN SHOW:	THE MACKINTOSH TROPHY	Given by Mrs G. Mackintosh
BEST OPPOSITE SEX:	THE KALO CUP	Given by Mrs B. & Miss K. Kidd
BEST PUPPY:	THE RONALD STEVENSON TROPHY	Given by Mr & Mrs K. Moore
BEST MINOR PUPPY:	THE HANNAH TURNER MEMORIAL TROPHY	Given by Mrs E. Lord
BEST JUNIOR:	THE FINNEYHALL TANKARD	Given by Mr & Mrs W. Higham

125

BEST NOVICE:	THE EMBAGES CUP	Given by Miss D. Mallins
GRADUATE BITCH:	THE TINICHARMS TROPHY	Given by Mr & Mrs Lindsey
BEST VETERAN	THE EMBAGES TROPHY	Given by Miss D. Malins
SPECIAL ELIMINATOR	THE KALO AWARD	Given by Miss K. Kidd

Three more new trophies given for September, 1989 from:

Mrs E. Dugen	REDROSE POLLY FLINDERS AWARD
Mr N. Johnston	DODDSLINE TROPHY
Mr & Mr Bevan	STARLOCH (HAELARBOBS) GRACIE FIELDS SHIELD

As well as the Annual Cups and Trophies on offer, there have been a considerable number of "Specials" generously donated at many of the Shows, which were won outright, for various classifications. Among those who kindly gave were:

Mrs W. Morphet	Mrs M. Webster	Mrs J. Ridley
Miss E. Lehtinen	Miss K. Kidd	Mr & Mrs W. Higham
Mr & Mrs Lindsey	Mrs I. Borlin	Mrs M. Magnusson

Rosettes have always been generously awarded by the Club, usually from first to fifth placings as well as many others. Since 1989 other Cups and Trophies have been added. For current list refer to Lancashire Heeler Club Secretary.

CHAMPIONSHIP SHOWS
WHERE LANCASHIRE HEELERS QUALIFYING
COULD APPEAR AT CRUFTS

After Blackpool scheduled the first Lancashire Heeler classes, gradually some other Championship Shows also put on a few Lancashire Heeler classes, which were welcomed by Lancashire Heeler exhibitors. These included Leeds, East of England, Scottish Kennel Club, Working Breeds Association of Wales, Working Breeds of Scotland, Ladies Kennel Association, Welsh Kennel Club and others joined the growing list, as each year passed. Where there were no Lancashire Heeler Classes, it meant entering in the Any Variety classes. Nevertheless, a considerable number of Lancashire Heelers found their way to Crufts Any Variety Classes, by qualifying during the years at general Championship Shows, (which was not particularly easy, often competing against better known breeds to many judges).

The first Lancashire Heeler to win a "First Card" (in Any Varieties Working) at Crufts was HAELARBOBS GRACIE FIELDS, owned by Mr & Mrs Bevan of Hastings and bred by Mrs Molly Old. On that day, 12th February, 1987, there were 26 Lancashire Heelers there and between them they collected 14 various cards. Judge was Mrs E. Bassett.

CRUFTS FIRST LANCASHIRE HEELER CLASSES

The following year, 1988, for the first time ever, Crufts scheduled 7 classes for Lancashire Heelers. The entry was 43 dogs making 61 entries. Judge was Mr Frank Jackson (of Lancashire). The Best of Breed was won by ACREMEAD BISCUIT OF KALO (a bitch), owned by Mrs Barbara and Miss Kathie Kidd and bred by Mrs Gwen Mackintosh. This made breed history by being the first Lancashire Heeler to represent the breed in the Working Group, and appear in Crufts Main Ring, which was televised. (It was fitting that for this very special occasion, Mrs Mackintosh was there to see a dog she had bred, win this honour, in view of the years she had devoted to pioneering the breed). (After the judging she shook hands with the judge, whom she had never met, and told him she agreed with his decision, not because she had bred the dog, but because in her opinion it was the right size, not too small and not too big!) The Sire of Acremead Biscuit of Kalo ("Jackie" as she was affectionately known) was Acremead Bogey and the Dam was Acremead Gigi.

The Reserve Best of Breed was the dog, BLACK DIAMOND OF FINNEYHALL, owned by Mr & Mrs W. Higham, and bred by Mr Norman Johnston. (Sire Pip of Doddsline and Dam was Cindy of Doddsline).

The Reserve Best Dog went to TUSHIELAW TOBY, owned by Mrs T. Allen and bred by Mrs D. Cargen.

The Reserve Best Bitch went to PEPI OF WINDER, owned by Mr & Mrs W. Morphet, and bred by Mrs S. Thompson.

WINNING DOGS AND EXHIBITORS AT THE FIRST LANCASHIRE HEELER CLASSES OF CRUFTS 1988

Saturday, 13th February, 1988

Judge: Mr Frank Jackson

SPECIAL PUPPY DOG (2)	OWNER:	BRED BY:
1. Foxthyme Pieces of Eight	Mrs M. Sharples	Mrs E. Lord
2. Sandpits Charlock	Mrs W. Lewis	Br. Exhibitor

POST GRADUATE DOG (9)		
1. Tushielaw Toby	Mrs T. Allen	Mrs D. Cargen
2. Doddsline Ben	Mr N. Johnston	Br. Exhibitor
3. Tushielaw Dougal at Nalu	Mrs D. Cargen	Br. Exhibitor
4. Stonebridge Ashley of Sandpits	Mrs W. Lewis	Mr S. Rozier
5. Elaine's Sam	Mr & Mrs K. Moore	Mr & Mrs W. Higham

OPEN DOG (13)		
1. Black Diamond of Finneyhall	Mr & Mrs W. Higham	Mr N. Johnston
2. Tushielaw Toby		
3. Tushielaw Clyde	Miss S. Whybrow	Mrs D. Cargen
4. Doddsline Ben		
5. Pip of Doddsline	Mr N. Johnston	Mrs Fisher

SPECIAL VETERAN DOG OR BITCH (1)		
1. Pepi of Winder	Mr & Mrs Morphet	Mrs S. Thompson

SPECIAL PUPPY BITCH (3)		
1. Doddsline Trudy	Mrs E. Adedeji	Mr N. Johnston
2. Sandpits Mazard	Mrs W. Lewis	Br. Exhibitor
3. Foxthyme Hidden Treasure	Mrs E. Lord	Br. Exhibitor

POST GRADUATE BITCH (18)		
1. Finneyhall Harvest Gold	Miss J. Spencer	Mr & Mrs Higham
2. Black Angel of Finneyhall	Mr & Mrs Higham	Mrs K. Draper
3. Kalo Quality Street	Mrs B. & Miss K. Kidd	Br. Exhibitors
4. Risehill Sophia	Miss S. Tickle	Br. Exhibitor
5. Chollagem Dolly Daydream	Mr & Mrs Belson	Br. Exhibitors

OPEN BITCH (15)

1. Acremead Biscuit of Kalo   Mrs & Miss Kidd   Mrs G. Mackintosh
2. Finneyhall Harvest Gold
3. Sandpits Earthsmoke   Mrs S. Lewis   Br. Exhibitor
4. Haelarbobs Gracie Fields   Mr & Mrs Bevan   Mrs M. Old
5. High Energy at Redrose   Mr & Mrs Higham   Mr N. Johnston

The following year on 10th February, Crufts again scheduled Lancashire Heeler Classes. This time they permitted two more classes being Limit Dog and Limit Bitch. (But owing to shortage of space at Crufts this time because of alteration work, the Kennel Club did not schedule any Puppy or Veteran Classes at all). So in 1989, Lancashire Heelers had 8 classes there. **43 dogs were entered making 63 entries. Judge was Mrs Ann Arch.**

PRINCIPAL WINNERS AT CRUFTS FOR 1989 WERE:

BEST OF BREED:
TUSHIELAW CLYDE
Owned by: Miss S. Whybrow
Bred by: Mrs D. Cargen

RESERVE BEST OF BREED:
MERRY MEG OF THE EMBAGES
Owned by: Miss D. Malins
Bred by: Mrs V. Hicks

RESERVE BEST DOG:
BLACK DIAMOND OF FINNEYHALL
Owned by: Mr & Mrs Higham
Bred by: Mr N. Johnston

RESERVE BEST BITCH:
BOUNCING BUBBLES
Owned by: Mrs A. C. Bowes
Bred by: Mrs E. M .L. Brady

THE FIRST LANCASHIRE HEELER TO BE
BEST OF BREED AT CRUFTS

This is the Bitch,
ACREMEAD
BISCUIT OF KALO

(Sire: Acremead Bogey
Dam: Acremead Gigi)

who made Breed History,
being the first ever
Lancashire Heeler to win
B.O.B. at Crufts 1988.
"Jackie" as she was
affectionately known
was the daughter of
Acremead Bogey
who was the first
Lancashire Heeler
to be applied for
for K.C. registration.

Photo by: E.M. LEHTINEN

Photo showing
the event on 13.2.1988,
with the judge
Mr Frank Jackson,
the owner,
Miss Kathie Kidd
and
Club President
Mrs Gwen Mackintosh.

Photo by: WENDY LEWIS

LIST OF CRUFTS'
BEST OF BREED WINNERS
There were no CCs until 1999

1988 ACREMEAD BISCUIT OF KALO (B)   *Judge: Mr Frank Jackson*
Owned by: Mrs B. & Miss K. Kidd
Bred by: Mrs G. Mackintosh

R.B.O.B. BLACK DIAMOND OF FINNEY (D)
Owned by: Mr & Mrs W. Higham
Bred by: Mr N. Johnston

1989 TUSHIELAW CLYDE (D)   *Judge: Mrs Ann Arch*
Owned by: Miss S. Whybrow
Bred by: Mrs D. Cargen

R.B.O.B. MERRY MEG OF THE EMBAGES (B)
Owned by: Miss D. Malins
Bred by: Mrs V. Hicks

1990 TUSHIELAW CLYDE (D)   *Judge: Mrs Pamela Cross-Stern*
Owned by: Miss S. Whybrow
Bred by: Mrs D. Cargen

R.B.O.B. MICHELMAS HOLLY OF BOWANNE (B)
Owned by: Mrs A. Bowes
Bred by: Mrs Brady

1991 TUSHIELAW CLYDE (D)   *Judge: Miss Kathie Kidd*
Owned by: Miss S. Whybrow
Bred by: Mrs D. Cargen

R.B.O.B. CHOLLAGEM LOVE 'N KISSES (B)
Owned & bred by: Mr & Mrs G. Belson

1992 DELSTEPS MADONNA (B) *Judge: Mr Harry Baxter*
Owned by: Mrs E. Lord
Bred by: Mrs M. S. Taylor

R.B.O.B. CHOLLAGEM HOPE 'N GLORY (D)
Owned by: Mrs C. Norman
Bred by: Mr & Mrs G. Belson

1993 TUSHIELAW CLYDE (D) *Judge: Mrs Joyce Cutbush*
Owned by: Miss S. Whybrow
Bred by: Mrs D. Cargen

R.B.O.B. DELSTEPS MADONNA OF FOXTHYME (B)
Owned by: Mrs E. Lord
Bred by: Mrs M. S. Taylor

1994 TUSHIELAW CLYDE (D) *Judge: Mr Robin Searle*
Owned by: Miss S. Whybrow
Bred by: Mrs D. Cargen

R.B.O.B. SARCASHA OCTOBER SUNRISE (B)
Owned by: Mr, Mrs & Miss Reich
Bred by: Miss S. Whybrow

1995 TUSHIELAW CLYDE (D) *Judge: Miss Jean Lanning*
Owned by: Miss S. Whybrow
Bred by: Mrs D. Cargen

R.B.O.B. KENINE MIDGE (B)
Owned by: Mr N. Sowerby
Bred by: Mr & Mrs W. Morphet

1996 FOXTHYME MATERIAL GIRL (B) *Judge: Mr Derek Smith*
Owned by: Mr & Mrs C. Russell
Bred by: Mrs E. Lord

R.B.O.B. FOXTHYME TOMSK (D)
Owned & bred by: Mrs E. Lord

1997 PATTERJO CANDY (B)   *Judge: Mrs Enid Lord*
Owned & bred by: Mrs J. Patrick

R.B.O.B. DODDSLINE LORD AT SWANNDALE (D)
Owned by: Mr & Mrs J. Swann
Bred by: Mr N. Johnston

1998 PATTERJO GINGHAM (B)   *Judge: Mr John Swann*
Owned & bred by: Mrs J. Patrick

R.B.O.B. TROUTOPS GORGEOUS GEORGE (D)
Owned & bred by: Mrs E. & Miss E. Gordon

1999 <u>**THE FIRST CCs AWARDED AT CRUFTS,**</u>
BOB & BITCH CC   *Judge: Mrs Ann Arch*
LAUSTEPH WALTZING MATILDA (B)
Owned & bred by: Mrs L. Martin

DOG CC
DODDSLINE KRISTEN (D)
Owned & bred by: Mr N. Johnston

2000 **BOB & BITCH CC**   *Judge:*
CH. FOXTHYME MATERIAL GIRL (B) *Mrs Zena Thorn-Andrews*
Owned by: Mr & Mrs C. Russell
Bred by: Mrs E. Lord

DOG CC
DODDSLINE LORD AT SWANNDALE (D)

2001 **BOB & BITCH CC**   *Judge:*
CH. FOXTHYME MATERIAL GIRL (B)   *Mr Norman Ziman*

DOG CC
CH. DODDSLINE LORD AT SWANNDALE (D)
Owned by: Mr & Mrs J. Swann
Bred by: Mr N. Johnston

2002 BOB & BITCH C.C.

TROUTOP GERALDINE (B)   *Judge: Mrs Enid Lord*

Owned by: Mrs E. & Miss E. Gordon

Bred by: Mrs E. & Miss E. Gordon

DOG C.C.

SIMSONSVILLE LIKELY LAD AT DUNCANDALE (D)

Owned by: Mr & Mrs B. Allison

Bred by: Mr & Mrs W. Simpson

THE FIRST CHAMPIONS IN THE U.K.

The first to gain the title in 1999 was CH. FOXTHYME MATERIAL GIRL (B).
Sire: Doddsline Ben Dam: Foxthyme Buttons & Bows.

Owned by: Mr Colin & Mrs Denise Russell

Bred by: Mrs E. Lord

The First
Champion
in the U.K.

**CH. FOXTHYME
MATERIAL GIRL**

Photo by:
RUSSELL FINE ART

THE FIRST CHAMPION DOG IN THE U.K.

Later the same year 1999 was CH. DODDSLINE KRISTEN. *Sire: Doddsline Lord at Swanndale Dam: Doddsline Lady Sarah.* Bred and owned by Mr Norman Johnston.

At the time of writing (May 2002) other Lancashire Heelers each with 2 CCs are:

BOWANNE YULE DELIGHT
Sire: Caesar Summer Solstice at Bowanne Dam: Bowanne Bits 'n Bobs
Bred by: Mrs Anne Bowes.
Owned by: Mr Tony & Mrs Gywn Hancock

LEONINE IVY OF RYSLIP
Sire: Ch. Doddsline Kristen Dam: Ryslip Bertha.
Bred by: Mrs J. Froggatt.
Owned by: Mrs J. S. Cartledge

YEDLIE BASIL AT BOWANNE
Sire: Foxthyme Tomsk Dam: Bowanne Tinkerbelle at Yedlie.
Bred & owned by: Mrs D. M. Lowe and Mrs L. Siggers.

JESTIKKA GLENORD
Sire: Foxthyme Orinoco Dam: Ch. Foxthyme Material Girl.
Bred & owned by: Mr C. M. & Mrs D. Russell.

FOXTHYME PLAYFUL KATE
Sire: Fredrick of Hoscar Dam: Foxthyme Play Away.
Bred & owned by: Mrs E. Lord

LAUSTEPH WALTZING MATILDA
Sire: Plaisance Peter Merle of Lausteph   Dam: Haelarbobs Mystic Megan of Lausteph.
Bred & owned by: Mrs L. Martin.

TUSHIELAW CLYDE
CRUFTS BEST OF BREED WINNER SIX TIMES

Photo by: SARAH WHYBROW

TUSHIELAW CLYDE was sired by Teddy Boy of Tushielaw and his dam was Kenee Jess of Tushielaw (bred by Mrs D. Cargen).

Owned by Miss Sarah Whybrow who handled him expertly and campaigned him winning many, many awards including Crufts BOB for the years 1989, 1990, 1991, 1993, 1994 & 1995.

Clyde was considered by many to be among the breeds most outstanding dogs having the desired conformation, a lovely temperament and in the ring possessed showmanship. During his show days the Kennel Club had not yet granted CCs for the breed, so sadly was denied the title of Champion in front of his name. But had CCs been on offer, he would have been a noteworthy champion, deserving the honour.

CRUFTS 1999 – THE FIRST SHOW TO AWARD CCs FOR LANCASHIRE HEELERS IN THE U.K.

CRUFTS 1999 the first year CCs were allocated for the Breed shows BOB winner LAUSTEPH WALTZING MATILDA with owner Mrs Laura Martin, who bred her, and judge Mrs Ann Arch holding the prized BOB Card and Rosette. Photo by: K. B. KIDD

Laura Martin and
LAUSTEPH
WALTZING MATILDA
receiving the
Kalo Shield for
BOB at Crufts from
Kathie Kidd
(who with the late
Mrs Barbara Kidd had
presented it in 1989).

Photo by: K. B. KIDD

137

THE VERY FIRST CHAMPION LANCASHIRE HEELERS GET THEIR TITLES IN SCANDINAVIA

As Challenge Certificates were not allocated to Lancashire Heelers in the U.K. until 1999, although a number have consistently won at Championship Shows, none could gain the coveted title.

But the first Champions for the breed gained their titles in Scandinavia (where the system is different from the U.K.)

The very first Lancashire Heeler to be made a Champion (Worldwide) was **DARLING MARLENE**, owned by Mrs Gunilla Schulze-Gustafson in SWEDEN, which was bred and exported by Mr A. Bray of Manchester. **CHAMPION DARLING MARLENE** was a **bitch**. (Born 15.1.84, out of Settanna Tango and Mighty Midge).

The first Lancashire Heeler **Dog** to become a Champion was owned by Miss Eeva-Maija Lehtinen in FINLAND. This was **CHAMPION ROSEADORE AMBASSADOR ANDY**, bred and exported by Mrs Dolly Rush. (Born 23.3.85, Sire: Acremead Solo and Dam: Acremead Buzz).

CH. DARLING MARLENE was SWEDISH & FINNISH CHAMPION - 8.11.1986 and added NORDIC CH. title 29.11.1986 and the news of ROSEADORE AMBASSADOR ANDY'S title was received in time to appear in the Lancashire Heeler Clubs December, 1987 Newsletter.

The first Lancashire Heeler to be exported (since the breed was K.C. recognised) was **Sandpits Black Mustard** (exported by Mrs Wendy Lewis) to Miss Eeva-Maija Lehtinen in Finland. Since then, Eeva had successfully made "Pretty" as she was known, into **CHAMPION SANDPITS BLACK MUSTARD**. (Sire: Stonebridge Ashley of Sandpits Dam: Stillastar Box of Trix of Sandpits).

But well before this, many years ago, in 1964, Mrs Mackintosh exported two to Chicago, in the U.S.A. to relations there (Now more are in the U.S.A.). These were not bred from (as they were both dogs!)

Now there are a lot of Lancashire Heelers in Sweden and Finland, as more have been exported. (Some are also in Continental countries). Also Miss Lehtinen was the first owner in Finland to breed a Lancashire Heeler litter. Whilst in Sweden Mrs Schulza-Gustafson was the first owner to do so. (See Chapter "Lancashire Heelers in Sweden).

THE VERY FIRST LANCASHIRE HEELER WORLDWIDE TO GAIN TITLE OF CHAMPION WAS CH. DARLING MARLENE. SHE WON HER FIRST CERTIFICATE AT SWEDISH K.C. CHAMPIONSHIP SHOW 18/5/86. (Judge: Violet Yates)

CH. DARLING MARLENE

Bred by Mr. A. Bray

Photo from:
MRS G. SCHULZE-GUSTAFSON

FINLANDS FIRST CHAMPIONS

Photo by: E. M. LEHTINEN

CH. ROSEADORE AMBASSADOR ANDY - Bred by Mrs. D. Rush

FINLANDS FIRST CHAMPIONS

*CH. SANDPITS
BLACK
MUSTARD*

"Pretty"

Bred by
Mrs. W. Lewis

Photo:
E.M. LEHTINEN

*CH. KALO
SUPER
SHADOW*

*Bred by:
Mrs B. &
Miss K.Kidd*

*Owned by:
Eeva Lehtinen*

Photo:
E.M. LEHTINEN

SUOMESSA REKISTERÖIDYT LANCASHIRE HEELERIT

1985 - 2000

E-ML

Above:
CHAMPION EIJATUUN
WELLCOME SANTA

Owner:
Eeva-Maija Lehtinen

Photo: E.M. LEHTINEN

Eeva-Maija Lehtinen >

LANCASHIRE HEELERS IN FINLAND 2000

In the year 2000 we had seven registered Lancashire Heelers. This pleased me because last year none were registered. There were 13 entries in official shows, and one Lancashire Heeler was seen in Agility games.

If you look at the registrations you can see that there is only one Finnish litter. It is easy to follow the Lancashire Heeler world here to see what has been happening because there aren't many Heelers in this country.

I have put all these dogs in alphabetical order:

Bitch Puppy ATOMOHI KYISHA (CH. Doddsline Lord at Swanndale – Swanndale Black Pearl at Atomohi) came to Rantalaukan kennel where "Mother" Sari Rantanen breeds Greyhounds. "Kiki's" breeders are A.D. & J.D. Smith, England.

HAGERBOS NOVA came from Sweden to Liisa Hynniselle, Helsinki. Dorothy Fursjo is her breeder.

And then the only Finnish litter is Sirpa Makelan's McHeel's "A" litter. (Dam: Perina and Sire: CH. Stardogs Sicke 'n Kiss). We have already seen all the four bitch puppies in the Puppy Class, Alicia, Ally-B, Amanda and Angelika.

Dog Puppy MOONGLADES SHROPSHIRE LASS "Elmo", came from Sweden. His breeder is Monica Wennerstrom, and his owner is Kirsi Hurskainen, Saarijarvi.

SHOW YEAR 2000

The Show Year began in January, we saw Lena Eliasson-Siversson with her imported dog Doddsline Kirk in Turki where the judge Rainer Vuorinen gave him the C.C. and B.O.B.

Eijatuun Victoria, owned by Rita Makineste was at Seinajoki's show and won 1/1 Res.C.C., BB1, B.O.B. Also she was at Oulu's show where she won 1/1. Agility games have been her "hobby" this year. She gained many excellent results, going from one class to another (from ALO to AVO) where she has already won very high results.

Moonglade's Shropshire Lass was shown twice, the first time to Saarijarvi where he was Best Puppy and at Jyvaskyla's show he won 2nd in the Junior Class.

At the show in Hameenlinna we saw all the McHeel's girls and their mother JMV-98 Perina (Junior World Winner). Best Puppy was 1. Amanda, 2. Angelika, 3. Ally-B, 4. Alicia. Perina won her last C.C. and so became a Finnish Champion. Her owner is Sirpa Makela.

At Somero's show, Lilian Hakkarainen's Finnish CH. Stardogs Va Du Vill "Piki", was BD1 and B.O.B. Eeva-Maija Lehtinen's bitch FIN. & EST. & LTU CH. LTUV-99 Eijatuun Wellcome Santa "Mari" was BB1 and B.O.S. A little while after this show Mari was in Latvia (one of the Baltic countries) where she won CEMPL1, CQ, LABK, CAC, CACIB and B.O.B. (You will know that the F.C.I. does not accept CACIB for Lancashire Heelers because as yet the F.C.I. does not recognise them). Mari won the title LACH (Latvia Champion).

We saw two new unregistered Heelers at the Puppy Shows, Doddsline Olga and Doddsline Ella, both of them won Best Puppy at different shows, owned by M. & M. Lahdekorpi.

At Helsinki's Winner 2000 Show were three Lancashire Heelers, Atomohi Kyisha 1/1 Junior Class and KP (Honour prize). This pleased her owners because "Kiki" won EVA. (At the show in Jyvaskyla she could not be judged as she had had an accident before showing and walked on three feet.

McHeel's Amanda won 2nd in Junior Class. The Best Lancashire Heeler was FIN. CH. Stardogs Va Du Vill who was B.O.B. and title winner 2000.

As we can see our Lancashire Heelers have been well shown and little "Viki", FIN. & N. CH. Eijatuun Victoria has also been doing Agility games.

More information can be obtained from the Yearbook 2000, available from Eeva-Maija Lehtinen, Vilniementie 3.A.2., 02940, Espoo, Finland. (This is the third edition, 1998, 1999 and 2000).

Eeva-Maija Lehtinen

FINLANDS LANCASHIRE HEELER REGISTER

1985 (2)
FIN MVA Sandpits Black Mustard
FIN MVA, V-91 Roseadore Ambassador Andy

1986 (1)
Kalo Birthday Prince

1987 (1)
FIN MVA Kalo Super Shadow

1988 (2)
Sandpits Charloc
Catellus Twiggy

1989 (5)
Catellus Uffe-Andersson
Catellus Urpo-Antinpoika
Catellus Uska Pikkulilli
Catellus Wenla
Catellus Vilma

1990 (6)
Cattelus Brown Surprise
Catellus Charlie Brown
Catellus Donna Colabella
Catellus Yucca Trademark
Catellus Yucon Hurricane
Catellus Your Busy-Lizzy

1991 (0)

1992 (1)
FIN & S & N & EST MVA, ESTV-93, V-95,-98
    Rallarrosens Milou

1993 (2)
Scarex Isac Chic 'n' Classy
Stardogs Free 'n' Clever

1994 (9)
Wiffy
FIN MVA Mongrels Fairy Fabiola
Mongrels Fair Fanny

Eijatuun Yo-Yo
Eijatuun Yazzy Long
Zorrera Andreas
Zorrera Andreotti
Zorrera Andros
Zorrera Andriano

1995 (0)

1996 (6)
FIN & EST; LTU & LA MVA, LTUV-99
    Eijatuun Wellcome Santa
Eijatuun Whippoorwil
Eijatuun Wonderful Casper
Snowqueen's Apple Jack
FIN MVA, V2000 Stardogs Va Di Vill
?

1997 (0)
Eijatuun Vackra Frösse
Eijatuun Via Valla
FIN & N MVA Eijatuun Victoria
Eijatuun Västervik
Paula
JMV-98, FIN MVA Perina
Snowqueen's Black Bami
Snowqueen's Black Beauty
Snowqueen's

1998 (2)
Mongrel's Pally-Pamela
Mongrel's Peeper-Paula

1999 (0)

2000 (7)
Atomohi Kyisha
Hägerbos Nova
McHeel's Alicia
McHeel's Ally-B
McHeel's Amanda
McHeel's Angelika
Moonglade's Shropshire Lass

CH. SANDPITS BLACK MUSTARD

CH. ROSEADORE AMBASSADOR ANDY

KALO BIRTHDAY PRINCE

CH. KALO SUPER SHADOW

SANDPITS CHARLOC

CATELLUS TWIGGY

Photo by: E.M. LEHTINEN

Photo by: E.M. LEHTINEN

CATELLUS BROWN SUPRISE

CATELLUS CHARLIE BROWN

CATELLUS URPO ANTINPOIKA

CATELLUS UFFE ANDERSSON

CATELLUS VENLA

CATELLUS BUSY LIZZY

CATELLUS DONNA COLABELLA

CATELLUS YUCON HURRICANE

CATELLUS YUCCA TRADEMARK

CH. SCAREX ISAC CHIC 'N' CLASSY

ZORRERA ANDREOTTI

STARDOGS FREE'N'CLEVER

CATELLUS USKA PIKKULILLI

WIFFY

RALLARROSENS MILOU

MONGRELS FAIRY FABIOLA

MONGRELS FAIR FANNY

EIJATUUN YO-YO

EIJATUUN JAZZY LONG

ZORRERA ANDREAS

SNOWQUEEN'S APPLE JACK

EIJATUUN WONDERFUL CASPER

EIJATUUN WHIPPOORWILL

CH. EIJATUUN WELLCOME SANTA

MONGRELS PEEPER PAULA

CH. STARDOGS VA'DU'VILL

EIJATUUN VICTORIA

PAULA

CH. PERINA

Photo by: R. MÄKINESTE

EIJATUUN VACKRA FRÖSSE

150

SNOWQUEEN'S BLACK BAMI

SNOWQUEEN'S BLACK BEAUTY

MONGRELS PALLY PAMELA

ATOMOHI KYISHA
Photo by: S. RANTANEN

McHEEL'S ALICIA
Photo by: S. MÄKELÄ

McHEEL'S ANGELIKA
Photo by: S. MÄKELÄ

McHEEL'S AMANDA
Photo by: S. MÄKELÄ

McHEEL'S ALLY-B
Photo by: S. MÄKELÄ

MOONGLADE'S SHROPSHIRE LASS
Photo by: K. HURSKAINEN

DODDSLINE ELLA

DODDSLINE OLGA
Photo by: M. LÄHDEKORPI

HÂGERBOS NOVA

**SWANNDALE
"FRANKIE"**

LANCASHIRE HEELERS
IN SWEDEN

The first Lancashire Heeler imported to Sweden 1984, when Gunilla Shulze-Gustaffson, well known Dachshund breeder kennel GISS imported the bitch Darling Marlene bred by J. Bray, England. Soon after this came the dog Tapatina Nippy-Noo who was Pat Taylor's breeding. The first Swedish bred litter was GISS litter (Tapatina Nippy Noo-Darling Marlene). In a short time they imported many new heelers from England to Sweden and the breeding started.

Dogs were imported from different kennels as: Chollagem, Embages, Sandpits Tushielaw, Finneyhall, Risehill and Stillastar. At the time of five first years saw the daylight, four Giss litters, Karin Tellander's Scarex puppies by (Doddsline Wilber Giss – Winder Double Gem), Jörgen Hellqvist's Ringhell's puppies (Embages Happy Harry – Giss Cest Ca) and Stardogs puppies (Doddsline Wilber Giss – Chollagem Rhythm 'n' Blue).

1989 was the year when they started the breed club which official name became Lancashire Heeler Club of Sweden. The first Chairman was Irene Börlin, Secretary Karin Tellandar and Treasurer Lena Eliasson-Siversson. The club magazine Lancashire Heeler Nytt began to appear four times in a year. Mongrels Lady Laura and Simson got the first CCs at the first official Club-Show which was held on August 17th, 1997.

Lancashire Heelers were seen in many different shows and the breed became more and more popular and some breeders went abroad to show their dogs. Giss breeding group was the first Heeler breeding group which were seen for the first time in Finland and it prized with honour prize. Also Tapatina Nippy-Noo and Darling Marlene had their own progeny classes. Because the differences in our show-rules, it was possible to get CCs at the Northern Countries and also get Champion titles, but then like at present it wasn't possible to get CACIB for the title of INTERNATIONAL CHAMPION because the breed wasn't FCI's breed.

The first Lancashire Heeler anywhere in the world to gain the Champion title 1986 was Ch. Darling Marlene (born 15.1.84 out of Settanna Tango and Mighty Midge [black & tan]).

Arileo's Cherie was the first liver/tan Champion in Sweden. Both Agility and Obedience has interested heeler owners and we have got some good results from them. To the year 2001 there are about 800 Lancashire Heelers now from the beginning.

The breed has been shown at the newspapers and at different kinds of shows. It has been possible to inform the breed in the best possible way in different places. The right information is very important to the public and to the Lancashire Heeler owners and breeders.

Eeva-Maija Lehtinen (from Lancashire Heeler Nytt 1985-2001)

* * *

Up to 2001 there were 111 Champions on the Swedish list. The system there to gain a title is different from the U.K. Regrettably space is limited to name them all here, but the list can be obtained from the Swedish Lancashire Heeler Club.

In 2002 Mrs Lena Eliasson-Siversson has written that her homebred Mongrel's First Fiona was the most winning Lancashire Heeler in Scandinavia. She is a Champion in Sweden, Finland, Denmark and Norway and has the titles Swedish Winner, Norwegian Winner, Kopenhagen Winner, Finnish Winner, Nordic Winner, International Winner, European Winner and World Winner.

THE LANCASHIRE HEELER
IN THE NETHERLANDS *by Dick Koster*

The breed is still very young in the Netherlands. The story in the Netherlands started only in late 1997 in a strange way. Our little mongrel had a car accident and we didn't expect her to survive in the end. So Trudi started to consider another small breed. A Havanese was first pick, but I wasn't too pleased with that. Then Trudi read a publication on the Lancashire Heeler in one of the major dog magazines and in the end gave me the choice: a Lancashire Heeler or a Havanese. The choice was clear for me...

Then the search started. I made contact with The Lancashire Heeler Club, talked about the breed and discussed options to see Heelers at shows and came to the conclusions that Crufts was the most attractive one. Sometime later we booked a flight to visit Crufts and meet the breed "live". After this acquaintance Trudi made up her mind and definitely chose a Lancashire Heeler.

So, in March 1998, Foxthyme Miss Marpeline (pet name Marple) came into our house and, as we found out a bit later, became the first Lancashire Heeler in the Netherlands. However, when we tried to register Marple, the Dutch KC refused to accept her because the FCI didn't recognise the breed. On the other hand the attitude of the Dutch KC was not negative. We started to contact them regularly to convince them to consider the Lancashire Heeler different from other breeds, but nothing changed: Heelers were not yet accepted by the Dutch KC and therefore not actively participating in the dog events.

In 1998 five other Heelers (all bitches) were imported. So, in the first year of their presence in the Netherlands, the number rose to six.

1999

Because our Kuvaszes considered Marple too small to be of any attractiveness, we started to consider importing a second one. So that was the way Foxthyme Captain Hastings came into our house. He arrived in February 1999 and was the first male Heeler in Holland.

In 1999 the Lancashire Heelers made two remarkable public appearances. The first was at the Kennel Clubs New Year Reception. Marple was introduced to some leading people and made a strong and very charming impression. The second event was at the Shepherd Show in Leiden. Marple and Hastings appeared at this Shepherd Show for the first time in public. For that occasion, I produced an information package and gave it the name The Heeler Herald. Several people showed interest and it was decided later to continue the Herald on a regular basis.

The number of owners was still small and there were only two imports in 1999 to welcome, but the number of interested people increased. However, the idea of how to proceed and try to get registration for the Lancashire Heeler was broadly accepted by all owners.

2000

A change was seen in 2000 when there was a bigger number of entries in our (private) registration. Eight puppies were registered, three of them even born in Holland. One of these imported dogs was imported from Sweden, the first from another country than England. In one year the number of Heelers doubled.

However, our Kennel Club still didn't register the breed. It seems to be a very unfamiliar situation that they had to cope with. Although there is still a positive attitude, there is nothing happening effectively. The owners, however, held some meetings and decided to continue with the attempts to introduce the breed in Holland. The Heeler Herald was designated the breed magazine.

2001

The year 2001 has been a special year in many ways. Twelve new dogs were registered (five born in Holland); this meant almost a doubling of the number of dogs. Furthermore, Foxthyme Miss Marpeline became Danish Champion and won a CAC in Oporto at the FCI-World Show(!); Hastings and Marple participated in the Club Show in Aspull and presented themselves very well – they qualified for Crufts.

In March, the Lancashire Heeler owners decided to found a Club. In June the Club (Fanciers and Breeders of the Lancashire Heeler in the Netherlands, LFLHN) started officially.

However, the situation with regard to registration remained vague. The Kennel Club got into a kind of internal crisis and had no intention nor time to put the Lancashire Heeler on her agenda. But as a signal for the positive intentions, one can consider the fact that the organisation of the World Show in Amsterdam decided to accept the Lancashire Heeler for a breed presentation. And in the meantime Marple became a regular guest at official Kennel Club meetings, like receptions and general meetings and is missed when not present.

Despite the fact that nothing happened with regard to the recognition, the support for the Lancashire Heeler increased. In 1999, we sent out about 10 copies of the Herald, in 2001 the number of subscriptions increased to more than 25. In the beginning of 2002 the counter indicated 35 memberships/subscriptions. This was also due to a publication in De Hondenwereld, the leading dog magazine in the Netherlands. The presentation of the breed at a local show even made the cover of the official Kennel Club magazine, the Kennel Gazet.

So in 4 years, the Lancashire Heeler made an impressive start, compared to other new breeds. The number of Heelers in Holland is 28, a club is founded in 2001 and many people joined it. The club magazine The Heeler Herald already counts three volumes. Discussions about the registration are ongoing, in the mean time the registration of the dogs is done by the club.

The majority of dogs has been imported from England. Several British kennels are represented here, Doddsline leading with seven dogs, and Swanndale and Foxthyme following with three each. There have been two dogs imported from Sweden (kennels Mongrel's and Moonglade's).

SOME LANCASHIRE HEELER STATISTICS

Confirmation that the Lancashire Heeler was recognised as a Pedigree Dog by the Kennel Club was written on 17th July, 1981 (Classified as a Rare Breed). It was in the Working Group. In 1999 Lancashire Heelers were transferred into the Pastoral Group.

The Lancashire Heeler Club was approved by the Show Regulation Committee (of the Kennel Club) at its Meeting on 8th March, 1983. Prior to 1981, no Lancashire Heelers were registered at the Kennel Club (being K.C. unrecognised and ineligible). But in 1981 just three were K.C. Registered, and from that date K.C. Registrations are as follows:

LANCASHIRE HEELERS REGISTERED AT THE KENNEL CLUB

1981	1982	1983	1984	1985	1986	1987	1988	1989	1990
3	41	87	90	124	113	133	160	231	222

1991	1992	1993	1994	1995	1996	1997	1998	1999	2000
136	165	172	180	138	167	222	208	182	164

The first Application the Kennel Club received to register a Lancashire Heeler was from Mrs Gwen Mackintosh, on 17th September, 1981, and it was for Acremead Bogey No. F00 96695 GO 2.

However, before Kennel Club recognition, a Lancashire Heeler Club was formed and at its Meeting on 1st July, 1978, the original Lancashire Heeler Standard was formulated and approved.

Also before K.C. recognition the Lancashire Heeler Club had its own system of Registering the dogs. This was for dogs of unregistered stock, but thought to be genuine specimens of the breed. Any such dogs had to be examined by a Lancashire Heeler Club approved Committee Member who had to assess the dogs according to the Lancashire Heeler Standard and all background information that could be known.

Those which appeared satisfactory were then permitted to be recorded on to the Lancashire Heeler Club register. When the Kennel Club recognised the breed it was a condition that those dogs being registered with the K.C. had first to be on the Lancashire Heeler Club register. Without this, the Kennel Club would not accept them. So to begin with, it meant that Lancashire Heelers had to be registered twice (firstly with the Lancashire Heeler Club Register, and then with the Kennel Club Register). BUT when Sires and Dams of progeny were already registered at the K.C. then it was possible to register the progeny direct with the K.C. (as is the custom for other pedigree breeds). Although the system was unusual (probably unique) it worked very well, as those who examined unregistered stock were instructed to be very particular, and not to "pass" if specimens appeared doubtful.

The Kennel Club at their meeting on 20th June, 1989, decided to close this system, and so as from 1st August, 1989, the Lancashire Heeler Club's own registrations ceased. This meant all Lancashire Heelers would register direct to the Kennel Club, as did other breeds. This applied to those with Dams and Sires already Kennel Club Registered.

It will be the case that in some places, a few good Lancashire Heeler specimens will exist, but were not registered before 1st August, 1989, they will never be eligible to claim pedigree status.

The number of Lancashire Heelers registered <u>on the Lancashire Heeler Club's</u> **OWN SYSTEM** as at April 1989 was 817.

Mrs Pam Welch was the original Lancashire Heeler Club Registration Secretary, and this was later taken on by Mrs Wendy Lewis. (The keeping of these records will prove so valuable to the History of the various Lines, as time passes).

**RARE BREED

The Kennel Club listed the Lancashire Heelers as a "Rare Breed" because so few were registered at the K.C. (or in fact registered anywhere). In fact, there are hundreds about (particularly around Lancashire and its immediate areas). But until the Breed was allocated Challenge Certificates it would be classed as a Rare Breed.

This changed in 1999, CCs were given for the first time at Crufts.

F.C.I. – (Federation Cynologique Internationale)

Despite the Lancashire Heeler being recognised by the British Kennel Club in 1981, as a Pedigree dog, up to time of writing, the F.C.I. (Headquarters in Belgium) have not recognised it in 1989. (Update April 2002 still unrecognised by F.C.I.)

Twice the F.C.I. have been approached (firstly in 1985 and again in 1989), but without success. They have been made aware of the situation, that the dog can be shown as a Pedigree. But it seems their criteria is different.

This means that in some Continental countries the Lancashire Heeler cannot take part in officially competitive Dog Shows. Therefore, anyone thinking of exporting to a potential buyer who wants to show, if they live on the Continent, it would be very wise first to enquire of their respective Country's Kennel Club, to know the exact current position. (This should apply to both exporter and importer).

DATES IN 'HEELER' HISTORY

1978 Meeting held to formulate the breed standard.

1978 First Newsletter circulated.

1981 Kennel Club finally recognised Lancashire Heeler as a pedigree dog on 17th July.

1981 Just three Lancashire Heelers registered at Kennel Club.

1982 First Championship Show scheduled Lancashire Heeler Classes was Blackpool.

1983 Lancashire Heeler Club finally approved by Kennel Club on 8th March.

1983 First Lancashire Heeler appeared at Crufts in AVNSC. (No Classes).

1984 First Lancashire Heeler Member's Limited Show held under Kennel Club Rules at Norfolk on 19th May.

1984 First Lancashire Heeler Open Show under Kennel Club Rules held near Preston on 16th October.

1985 First Eye-testing took place at Norfolk Show (All tested there, CLEAR).

1986 First Lancashire Heeler to gain Champion title in Sweden was Darling Marlene.

1987 First Lancashire Heeler won a RED CARD in AVNSC at Crufts. (Haelarbobs Gracie Fields).

1987 First Champion title in Finland won by Roseadore Ambassador Andy.

1988 First time Lancashire Heeler Classes at Crufts, Best of Breed Acremead Biscuit of Kalo.

1988 Lancashire Heeler Club celebrated its tenth anniversary. President Mrs Gwen Mackintosh presented silver tankard to be shared between Norfolk and Lancashire Shows.

1989 Kennel Club closed Lancashire Heeler Club's own registration system (approx. 817 dogs).

1989 Sweden started the first Lancashire Club outside the U.K.

1989 Crufts Best of Breed winner Tushielaw Clyde held this for SIX years.

1990 Sweden held its first Specialty Show.

1990 First Lancashire Heeler book published.

1996 Meeting held to form another breed club, known as The East of England (proposed) Lancashire Heeler Club (unofficial).

1999 Lancashire Heelers cease to be classed as a rare breed.

1999 Lancashire Heelers transferred into Pastoral Group from Working.

1999 First CCs to be awarded to Lancashire Heelers at Crufts.
Bitch CC - **Lausteph Waltzing Matilda** - B.O.B. Judge: Mrs Anne Arch
Dog CC - **Doddsline Kristen**

1999 The Colour Liver and Tan to be permitted also for Lancashire Heelers and included in Standard.

1999 The First Champion in the U.K. was Ch. Foxthyme Material Girl (Bitch)

1999 The First Champion dog in the U.K. was Ch. Doddsline Kristen.

2001 The First Lancashire Heeler accepted to the American Kennel Club Foundation Stock Service Registry on August 1st, 2001 was Pennijar Pilgram.

2002 The First Lancashire Heeler to become an Irish Champion was Telpoolwyn Ashraf.

IS THE LANCASHIRE HEELER
A HEALTHY BREED?
Eye Problems

When choosing a dog everyone hopes it will be with them for a long time, enjoying good health. Many breeds, however, seem to have a dominant potential weakness, Hip Dysplasia is well known for some as one such concern.

But generally Lancashire Heelers were thought to be relatively healthy until some eye problems happened which are being monitored and studied carefully in the hope that with time, the problems may be eradicated.

It is only fair in a book of this nature to be open about the subject so that prospective owners are aware of the situation. Having said that, many dogs are problem free and personally I would not be deterred from choosing a Lancashire Heeler as a companion.

When buying one, it's very important to ask the seller to show the current Eye Testing Certificate for the puppy, its Mother and Father (and even Grandparents if possible).

An in depth study with explanations of the various conditions has been kindly contributed by Miss Jacky Cutler, which states the position as known in May, 2002.

EYE PROBLEMS – by Jacky Cutler

As with many other breeds the Lancashire Heeler has its share of eye problems.

The B.V.A./K.C./I.S.D.S. Eye Scheme offers a means of identifying and investigating the presence of inherited eye diseases. They appoint a panel of specialists to carry out eye testing on dogs of all ages and breeds.

Dogs do not have to be clinically affected to pass on certain conditions; they may be 'carriers' whilst showing no signs themselves.

Conscientious breeders recognise the need for testing any dog, which is to be used for breeding, and the subsequent examination of the litter before twelve weeks of age. Buyers should ask to see current eye testing certificates for the mother and puppies (and father if possible) and should be informed of the need for continued testing throughout the life of the dog in order to allow monitoring and any hereditary problems in the breed.

There are at present four conditions under investigation in Lancashire Heelers:

1. Hereditary Cataract (H.C. early developing). Cataracts can have several causes and a small number are believed to be hereditary. Clinical features are opacity (clouding) of the lens.

161

2. Persistant Pupillary Membrane (P.P.M.) During the last three weeks of fetal development tissue which protects the pupil begins to degenerate naturally and in most cases has disappeared completely by six weeks of age.

   Persistence of the pupillary membrane is a common phenomenon in many breeds. Puppies which test positive are sometimes found to be clear when retested at a later stage. Clinical signs are strands of tissue remaining visible in the eye.

3. Collie Eye Anomaly (C.E.A.). Whilst mainly affecting the collie breeds, cases have been identified in Heelers. It is a congenital condition (i.e. present at birth) which produces lesions on the surface of the eye, and can be diagnosed at five to six weeks. The majority of dogs show no apparent visual defect, but it would be wise to avoid breeding from affected dogs.

4. Primary Lens Luxation (P.L.L.). This is by far the most serious of the four conditions as it can cause persistent pain and blindness. Although there is no actual test to determine whether a dog is affected, some cases have been detected when presented for eye testing. If found at a very early stage the lens can be removed, leaving approximately 40% of vision, although secondary glaucoma may be unavoidable leaving the eye totally blind. When one eye is affected, the other invariably follows, sometimes almost immediately but often some months later.

   This condition usually occurs between three and seven years. The suspensory ligaments holding the lens in place degenerate and allow the lens to move and fluid to build up.

Affected dogs should not knowingly be bred from, although without a D.N.A. test it is impossible to know which dogs are going to be affected, clear or carriers of the condition.

Owners should regularly check their dogs eyes for any signs of abnormality or discomfort, which should be inspected by a vet without delay, who may refer the case to an eye specialist for further investigation and treatment.

Further information on any of the above conditions is available from:

BRITISH VETERINARY ASSOCIATION
7 MANSFIELD STREET, LONDON W1M 0AT

or

ANIMAL HEALTH TRUST
LANWADES HALL, NEWMARKET, SUFFOLK CB8 7DW

GESTATION TABLE

Which at a glance shows when a bitch is due to whelp.

Average duration is 63 days, but this can vary with different bitches and with different breeds. Some smaller breeds can be earlier.

SERVED JANUARY	DUE TO WHELP MARCH	SERVED FEBRUARY	DUE TO WHELP APRIL	SERVED MARCH	DUE TO WHELP MAY	SERVED APRIL	DUE TO WHELP JUNE	SERVED MAY	DUE TO WHELP JULY	SERVED JUNE	DUE TO WHELP AUGUST	SERVED JULY	DUE TO WHELP SEPTEMBER	SERVED AUGUST	DUE TO WHELP OCTOBER	SERVED SEPTEMBER	DUE TO WHELP NOVEMBER	SERVED OCTOBER	DUE TO WHELP DECEMBER	SERVED NOVEMBER	DUE TO WHELP JANUARY	SERVED DECEMBER	DUE TO WHELP FEBRUARY
1	5	1	5	1	3	1	3	1	3	1	3	1	2	1	3	1	3	1	3	1	3	1	2
2	6	2	6	2	4	2	4	2	4	2	4	2	3	2	4	2	4	2	4	2	4	2	3
3	7	3	7	3	5	3	5	3	5	3	5	3	4	3	5	3	5	3	5	3	5	3	4
4	8	4	8	4	6	4	6	4	6	4	6	4	5	4	6	4	6	4	6	4	6	4	5
5	9	5	9	5	7	5	7	5	7	5	7	5	6	5	7	5	7	5	7	5	7	5	6
6	10	6	10	6	8	6	8	6	8	6	8	6	7	6	8	6	8	6	8	6	8	6	7
7	11	7	11	7	9	7	9	7	9	7	9	7	8	7	9	7	9	7	9	7	9	7	8
8	12	8	12	8	10	8	10	8	10	8	10	8	9	8	10	8	10	8	10	8	10	8	9
9	13	9	13	9	11	9	11	9	11	9	11	9	10	9	11	9	11	9	11	9	11	9	10
10	14	10	14	10	12	10	12	10	12	10	12	10	11	10	12	10	12	10	12	10	12	10	11
11	15	11	15	11	13	11	13	11	13	11	13	11	12	11	13	11	13	11	13	11	13	11	12
12	16	12	16	12	14	12	14	12	14	12	14	12	13	12	14	12	14	12	14	12	14	12	13
13	17	13	17	13	15	13	15	13	15	13	15	13	14	13	15	13	15	13	15	13	15	13	14
14	18	14	18	14	16	14	16	14	16	14	16	14	15	14	16	14	16	14	16	14	16	14	15
15	19	15	19	15	17	15	17	15	17	15	17	15	16	15	17	15	17	15	17	15	17	15	16
16	20	16	20	16	18	16	18	16	18	16	18	16	17	16	18	16	18	16	18	16	18	16	17
17	21	17	21	17	19	17	19	17	19	17	19	17	18	17	19	17	19	17	19	17	19	17	18
18	22	18	22	18	20	18	20	18	20	18	20	18	19	18	20	18	20	18	20	18	20	18	19
19	23	19	23	19	21	19	21	19	21	19	21	19	20	19	21	19	21	19	21	19	21	19	20
20	24	20	24	20	22	20	22	20	22	20	22	20	21	20	22	20	22	20	22	20	22	20	21
21	25	21	25	21	23	21	23	21	23	21	23	21	22	21	23	21	23	21	23	21	23	21	22
22	26	22	26	22	24	22	24	22	24	22	24	22	23	22	24	22	24	22	24	22	24	22	23
23	27	23	27	23	25	23	25	23	25	23	25	23	24	23	25	23	25	23	25	23	25	23	24
24	28	24	28	24	26	24	26	24	26	24	26	24	25	24	26	24	26	24	26	24	26	24	25
25	29	25	29	25	27	25	27	25	27	25	27	25	26	25	27	25	27	25	27	25	27	25	26
26	30	26	30	26	28	26	28	26	28	26	28	26	27	26	28	26	28	26	28	26	28	26	27
27	31	27	May 1	27	29	27	29	27	29	27	29	27	28	27	29	27	29	27	29	27	29	27	28
28	Apr 1	28	2	28	30	28	30	28	30	28	30	28	29	28	30	28	30	28	30	28	30	28	Mar 1
29	2	29	3	29	31	29	July 1	29	31	29	31	29	30	29	31	29	31	29	31	29	31	29	2
30	3			30	Jun 1	30	2	30	Aug 1	30	Sep 1	30	Oct 1	30	Nov 1	30	Dec 1	30	Jan 1	30	Feb 1	30	3
31	4			31	2			31	2			31	2	31	2			31	2			31	4

DON'T PANIC

(A Guide to Whelping, Rearing and Selling Puppies)

BY WENDY LEWIS

Before embarking on breeding a litter of puppies it is as well to ask yourself one or two questions; bearing in mind the fact that most dog rescue homes are overflowing with unwanted dogs, many of whom have been cruelly treated.

Why do you want a litter? – If the answer is 'because it would be good for the bitch', then do not bother to mate her. She will be perfectly happy as long as you love and care for her, and never realise that she has missed anything.

Another frequently heard reason is that 'it will settle the bitch down'. It won't. I have never known having a litter to change a bitch's basic temperament. A jittery, sharp bitch will probably become fiercer when all her protective instincts are aroused.

Do NOT embark on a litter if you are not going to be at home all day to care for them. Many things could go disastrously wrong while you are away.

Rearing a litter is time consuming and expensive; don't expect to make money out of it. There are many hidden costs such as vets bills, electricity, soap powder etc.

DO make sure you have some homes lined up for your puppies ... genuine ones. You will find that most of the friends and relatives who would 'love one of dear Flossy's puppies', suddenly find good reasons why they can't have one when your puppies are four to five weeks old. They tend to move house or leave the country, or find some member of the family who is allergic to dogs.

Having established that your reasons for breeding a litter are sound, and that you have the time to devote to the exercise, you will be looking for a Stud dog.

THE STUD DOG

A fair amount of consideration should be given to your choice of a Stud dog. It is not a good idea to rush to the top winning dog in your breed, unless he carries the characteristics which will compliment those of your bitch and, hopefully, produce puppies which are as good as, or better than, their parents.

It is of vital importance that the dog of your choice should be of sweet, amenable temperament. It is very unlikely that many of the resulting litter will enter the show ring, therefore most of them will become pets. The prime qualities for a pet should be a sound healthy animal of good temperament, with no inherited abnormalities.

The quick way to the top in the show ring, seems to be to mate close relatives to 'fix' type. This can work, but it will also accentuate any faults, seen or unseen, and does tend to reduce the size of the animal.

A mating of distant relatives is called Line-Breeding. A mating of close relatives such as Father/Daughter or Brother/Sister is called In-Breeding and should only be undertaken by very knowledgeable people, and even then is of very doubtful value.

I have mated a Father to a Daughter in a breed where everything in the pedigrees was a complete outcross. The result was two dogs and two bitches. One dog was very small and highly strung. The other, though very nice, was a unilateral cryptorchid (only one testicle descended). One bitch which was humanely destroyed at two days old, and on post mortem was found to have a deformed intestine. The other bitch had the worst overshot mouth I have even seen. This litter definitely put me off breeding with closely related dogs.

I started to breed dogs in an old established breed, and after five years had managed to acquire most of the inherited faults of that breed, after quite a good start.

Eventually, although I could produce dogs which would win in the show ring, I did not want to breed from them because I knew there were faults in other members of the same litter. Also, the Kennel Club Breed Standard for this breed read 'long, low and level' which is a recipe for spinal problems, severe pain for the dogs, and much heartache for owners.

Over a period, loving pet homes were found for most of my small kennel (the oldies stayed with me), and I took up a newly recognised rare breed which had not been inbred and was still full of hybrid vigour.

At the first Breed Show I attended, out of the thirty dogs entered, only two or three looked alike. In the 15 years in which I have been watching this breed, the dogs are beginning to conform much more to a standard, but problems have now arisen because in the early days too many bitches were mated to one top winning dog.

Although this produced very nice looking puppies, it has now reduced the gene pool significantly, which has resulted in a lack of good sires which could be used as an outcross.

Anyway, back to your Stud dog, chosen we hope for his good temperament as well as his beauty.

Contact the dog's owner BEFORE your bitch comes into season and make the arrangements for her to visit him. If you do not already know it, ask for a copy of the dog's pedigree which you can then compare with your bitch's.

When your bitch comes into season, worm her, but do not worm her again after she has been mated until about four weeks after the birth of her puppies.

If you keep several bitches, you may find that they will all come into season at around the same time. If this happens, keep a close eye on any unmated bitch whose season coincided with your pregnant bitch. The unmated one may probably show signs of having milk about eight weeks after her season, and should anything go wrong with your whelping it may be possible to stimulate her milk to foster the puppies.

A very maternal Miniature Dachshund of mine who was busy guarding an imaginary litter in her bed, reared, very successfully, five Standard Dachshund puppies for a friend whose bitch had picked up rat poison and died the night she had the puppies.

In packs of wild dogs, it is natural for unmated bitches to produce milk and feed the puppies while the dam is out hunting.

Inform the stud dog's owner when your bitch first comes in season and arrange the date for her visit: this will usually be eleven or twelve days after you have first noticed she is bleeding.

If you have to travel a long way to the dog of your choice, the twelfth day may be the best. If you can manage two matings, do them on the tenth and twelfth days. That way you should have viable sperm in the bitch for a period of four days.

If you keep other dogs, your bitch will show when she is ready to be mated, by flirting with them and standing with her tail curled over to one side, inviting them to mount her.

THE MATING
It is usual practice for the bitch to travel to the dog's home for the mating. On arrival, the first thing you should do is take her for a short walk in case she needs to empty herself.

Then, if she hasn't taken an instant dislike to the dog, allow them a short period of flirtation, off the lead if possible, to relax her. Not too long or the dog may 'run out of puff'.

If she does decide she hates him, one can achieve a mating with a keen dog by tying the bitch's mouth with a bandage, to stop her biting, and holding her firmly for the dog. Large breeds may present more of a problem. A diffident dog may be put off completely by a snapping and snarling bitch.

I am not really in favour of rape in the cases. I have done it, but things have tended to go wrong at the other end of the pregnancy.

One owner and I spent most of a day trying to mate her reluctant bitch to one of my stud dogs, and finally achieved it in the evening. She duly whelped two puppies, but the bitch died two days later.

Another bitch which I had mated against her will had a long, protracted whelping which was really a case of partial inertia. After these two experiences, if any bitch was adamant that she didn't want to be mated, I decided to trust to her instinct that she knew things that I didn't.

Sometimes a bitch will accept one dog quite happily, but refuse another, again there is probably a very good reason why, so I don't force the issue.

Presuming all is going well, the dog will mount the bitch and they will tie. Once tied, the dog may turn so that they face away from each other. This is probably a defensive measure should they be attacked whilst relatively helpless. At least there are two sets of teeth facing outwards.

They will remain tied throughout the mating. Usually a tie lasts for about 20 minutes, it can be shorter. It can also be much longer: I had two dogs once which tied for two and a half hours during which time the dog went to sleep twice. I had to break it up eventually by putting towels under the dogs and pouring cold water on the relevant bits.

The first part of the dog's ejaculation carries the sperm, and the subsequent fluid washes it through. Consequently it is perfectly possible to get a pregnancy if the pair do not tie, provided the dog has entered the bitch for a minute or two.

It is best to gently hold both dogs steady whilst they are tied. A jittery bitch could possibly harm the dog and I know of one dog which died of a ruptured spleen after mating a difficult bitch.

After the mating, the stud dog's owner should give you a copy of the dogs pedigree, which you will need in the future to write out the pedigrees for your puppies. You should also be given a Kennel Club Litter Registration Form with the stud dog's section completed, giving his Kennel Club Registration Number.

The dog's owner should give you a receipt for the stud fee. Most owners will offer a free return to that dog if your bitch does not become pregnant, but this is not obligatory. What you are paying for is the actual mating on the day and the stud fee is not returnable if your bitch does not become pregnant.

167

Should this happen, it is most unlikely to be the stud dog's fault. Some bitches do not follow the usually accepted norm of being at maximum fertility on day eleven or twelve of their season. I have had one which became pregnant from an unplanned mating on day two, and another on day twenty-two, when it should have been safe to let her back in with the pack; but this is unusual.

CARE OF THE PREGNANT BITCH

About three weeks after the mating, your bitch may seem to be a little 'off colour', which will be a promising sign that she is pregnant. You should be able to confirm this at about five weeks as, when viewed from above, she will be seen to be thickening at the waistline. At seven weeks you should be able to see and feel the pups move.

Birth normally takes place on or about the 63rd day of pregnancy. There is remarkably little variation in this gestation length, therefore if your bitch goes more than two days over this time, you should seek veterinary advice in case there is a problem.

During the pregnancy, follow exactly the same routine and feed the bitch as you did before. Don't start adding all sorts of exotic foods and vitamin pills to her diet; you are in danger of doing more harm than good. If she has always looked fit and well on her normal diet, then stick to it. Her body has enough to do with adjusting to the pregnancy, without having to cope with unfamiliar foods.

The most important thing with the breeding of any animals is to observe them carefully. If they look bright eyed, fit and well in their coats, they are getting all they need.

Keep up the exercise right until the day she whelps. She will naturally slow up a bit towards the end, but all my bitches have come on normal walks all the way through pregnancy.

This can also be quite a good guide to when she is about to whelp. You will find that she is not keen to go far from home the day before she goes into labour and will try to go back to where she has decided to produce her litter.

Try to fix in the bitch's mind, at least a week before the puppies are due, that the whelping box is the best place to have them. Under the garden shed can give you heart failure and if she gets it into her head that your bed is ideal, you may have a hectic whelping chasing her upstairs every time there is a puppy coming; even when they are all born and nicely settled in the whelping box, you will find she still keeps going back to the place where SHE had decided to have them.

Around the fifth to sixth week of pregnancy you can increase the bitch's daily food ration by about 10 per cent, unless she is too fat anyway, in which case it is best to use the pregnancy to slim her a bit. A lean fit bitch will have an easier, quicker, whelping than a fat lazy one. The fat one will have layers of fat internally as well as externally, and this will impede the passage of the pups and make the uterus sluggish.

The sixth to seventh week increase the ration again by 10 per cent, and so on each week until she whelps. Don't overdo the food in the last two weeks as this is when the pups really begin to grow, and enormous pups will give a difficult whelping.

Every day for the last week prior to whelping, give the bitch calcium tablets, dosing according to size. This is to try to ensure that there will be enough calcium in the system for the actual birth. Remember she has had to use calcium to build the puppies skeletons. After she has whelped, increase the dose, spreading it over the day, all the time that she is producing milk for the puppies. This is to try to prevent Eclampsia, which can be a killer.

ECLAMPSIA is caused by a sudden demand on the bitch's calcium supply resulting in the bitch depriving herself of her own blood calcium to put into the milk. This usually happens after the puppies are born, but I do know of someone who lost a bitch with it the day before she should have whelped seven puppies. The owner didn't realise what was wrong.

SYMPTOMS OF ECLAMPSIA are as follows:

The bitch will seem unhappy and uncomfortable and may start to pant. Her head may begin to shake like someone with Parkinsons disease. She may go lame or off her legs altogether. If you put a hand on her you will be able to feel her muscles jumping and twitching.

IT IS VITAL THAT YOU TAKE HER STRAIGHT TO THE VET no matter the time of day or night, or she will die.

Depending on how far the Eclampsia has progressed the vet will either give her two injections; one intra-muscular for a more rapid effect, and another sub-cutaneous one for long acting effect. If the bitch is in danger of going into convulsions, which is the next stage, the vet will administer an intravenous injection of calcium which can have an almost magically instantaneous effect, though don't worry if it doesn't.

If you have gone straight to your vet at the first signs of eclampsia, your bitch has every chance of surviving, but do not waste any time in doing so.

Your vet may then suggest that you take the bitch away from the puppies and hand rear them. This is fine in theory, but virtually impossible in practice as your bitch will be utterly miserable and make sure that you are too.

I compromise until the pups are eating and drinking by themselves at around four weeks, by leaving the bitch with them but watching her like a hawk all day and either having her in my bed at night, with two trips out to feed the puppies. Or sleeping fitfully on the floor beside the whelping box. It's exhausting, but doesn't go on for long.

A clear whitish discharge may be seen during the last few weeks of pregnancy, this is normal and nothing to worry about. Should you at any stage of the pregnancy see a black or greenish discharge you will need veterinary assistance as probably one of the puppies has died in the uterus.

WHELPING EQUIPMENT

1)   Whelping Box (well disinfected)
2)   Newspapers
3)   Two Vet Beds (Special synthetic furry washable pads)
4)   Dull Emitter Heat Lamp
5)   Heated Pad
6)   Pair of Blunt Scissors
7)   Artery Clamp
8)   Sewing Cotton and Iodine
9)   Several Towels and a Flannel
10)   Cardboard Box
11)   Hot Water Bottle

Finally, and probably most important, a large flask of hot coffee. Veterinary advice on this is the flask should also contain brandy.

The Whelping Box should be large enough to give the bitch and pups room to move about. Ideally it should be possible to have the sides low for the actual delivery so that one can reach the bitch comfortably should assistance be needed. Then the sides will need to be heightened (or perhaps another box) so that it can be covered and darkened for two or three weeks after the pups are born.

This makes the box warmer, draught free and nearer to the natural conditions of earth or cave which the bitch would have chosen for herself. When whelping is imminent take care that she doesn't disappear under the garden shed which may have to be dismantled to retrieve her.

The Whelping Box should have a wooden rail round the inside measuring 2.5cm x 2.5cm (1in x 1in). This is fixed to the side of the box on blocks so that it projects into the box by about 5cm (2in) at a height of about 7.5cm (3in) from the floor of the box. This will ensure that when the pups creep round behind their mum, as they invariably do during the first week of life, they will not be suffocated by her lying on them.

Place a pad of newspaper on the floor of the box and cover this with a piece of Vet Bed cut to fit the box. During the whelping I use a Dull Emitter Heat lamp over the box because it is useful for warming slow puppies as you are massaging life into them. The newspaper will soak up any fluid which will pass straight through the Vet Bed.

When whelping is completed, remove the newspaper, change to a heated pad under a clean Vet Bed and remove, or switch off the overhead Dull Emitter Lamp unless it is particularly cold. If leaving it on, do make sure that there is a cool part of the box which the bitch and whelps can escape to if they get too hot.

The Blunt Scissors are for severing tough umbilical cords. Sharp scissors give too clean a cut which tends to bleed more. Remember this job is usually done by the bitch's teeth.

The Artery Clamp is to clamp to the afterbirth end of the cord if the afterbirth is still retained by the bitch after you have detached the puppy. This will hold the afterbirth until the bitch is ready to deliver it easily and stop it slipping back into the uterus.

The Towels are for drying puppies, and the Flannel for holding slippery puppies for an assisted delivery.

The Cardboard Box containing the Hot Water Bottle with a folded Vet Bed on top is for the first born pups to keep them warm and safe while the next one arrives... as long as the bitch does not mind you removing them. Don't have a battle with her over this, if she gets very distressed when you move them, it is safer to leave them with her and take the small risk of them getting stepped on. You can usually sneak them away just as the next one is appearing and taking all her attention.

THE WHELPING

I am not going to go into all the possible problems which can arise during a whelping as there are plenty of books which describe these. Most of them require veterinary assistance which you will have summoned when you felt that things were not proceeding normally; but I would just mention INERTIA.

If your bitch has reached her due date but nothing seems to be happening, do not let her go more than two days past that date without having her checked by the vet. Sometimes, if there are only one or two puppies, they may not produce enough of the hormone needed to trigger the fall of progesterone levels to precipitate the whelping.

In cases of inertia you can usually detect subtle changes in your bitch if you know her well. I have known one who just sat around looking worried.

There can also be partial inertia where the bitches body is not really working hard enough to expel the puppies. Although she may be having visible muscular contractions, the uterus may not be contracting. This could be caused by the bitch being overweight and under-exercised. There is also a school of thought that believes it could be an hereditary problem. It is as well before breeding from your bitch to ask for a history of her dam's whelping.

I cannot stress too much, how important it is to have your bitch lean and fit before the mating. It can save a lot of later problems. If your bitch is too fat it is better to put off having a litter for six months and work on her fitness during that time.

If you think that whelping is imminent, but are not sure, your best course is to take the bitches temperature. The foetuses determine the time of whelping by triggering a fall in the level of the hormone progesterone in the bitch. This in turn causes a drop in the body temperature. This lowering of temperature normally occurs 24 to 28 hours before the bitch goes into labour. The normal temperature of 101.5 will drop to around 98 degrees.

The bitch will most probably go off her food and begin to scratch up her bedding to make a nest. If you sit and watch her flanks at this stage you may be able to see the horns of the uterus contracting into a hard ridge, while she bedmakes to take her mind off the pain. The pups lie in the horns of the uterus which run up each side of the bitch's flanks.

She will not have begun to push yet as the cervix will not be dilated enough to deliver the puppies. She may also be sick at this stage of the proceedings.

There will be a discharge of mucus: this is the plug which sealed the neck of the womb, coming away.

As soon as the cervix is fully opened, the bitch will go into the second stage of labour and will begin to push with each contraction. This stage seems to bother them less than the first and once they settle down to work, they seem to know what to expect at the end of it.

Look at your watch when you see the first actual push by the bitch. Most books on the subject will say that if you have not got a puppy in two hours from that time you may need assistance. If your bitch is a maiden and the straining seems normal with rests in between, and she is not too distressed I generally wait a little longer... it rather depends how far from your vet you live.

It is a good idea to let your vet know anyway when your bitch goes into labour so that he is primed should you need him later. As a matter of courtesy, don't forget to let him know afterwards that all has gone well.

If the bitch is straining continuously and seems in a lot of pain, after two hours without producing anything, something may be wrong.

At some stage the first water bag will appear and after a push or so will burst. Do not touch or burst this yourself as it is designed to gently dilate the passage for the puppies. You may not see this but will find the bitch is very interested in a wet patch in the bed.

The next water bag to appear should contain a puppy, there is a water bag with each puppy. You will see the end of the bag appear. Do not touch it or interfere at all. Quite often if the pup is half out, the urge to help may be overwhelming. But control this urge. A few more pushes will deliver the pup naturally, whereas if you pull it you may hurt the bitch and she will probably stop pushing and may even try to get out of the whelping box to get away from the pain.

The time to assist the birth is usually if you can see the pup is coming backwards; that is with the tail and hind feet showing. This presentation is not unusual but may take the bitch longer to push out. Don't interfere unless you think she is really struggling to get it out.

In all the litters I have delivered, just under half the pups were posterior presentation. This is not a breech birth.

A breech birth is when you are presented with the pups bottom only with the hind legs still forward. I have never had this situation, but would suggest that you wait until the bitch stops pushing, then between pushes, try to ease the pup back inside her, find the back legs, and bring them back into the correct position.

When assisting a posterior presentation, take hold of what you can of the pup with a clean flannel, (they are very slippery) and as the bitch pushes, ease the pup, very gently, in a curve, down, round and underneath the bitch between her hind legs. This is the natural direction for the birth.

Never pull straight out, and don't pull when the bitch is not straining.

Most of all DON'T PANIC: it won't help, the bitch will sense it and it will take her mind off the job.

When the pup is delivered, you can leave the bitch to free it from the membrane if she seems to know what to do. I must admit here that I don't... all that chewing and pulling on the umbilical cord worries me, and can leave your pups with umbilical hernias. I lost a pup once with peritonitis because the bitch had chewed the cord off right against the pup and infection had set in.

Some bitches seem to start chewing through the cord before freeing the pup from the membrane and become more interested in the afterbirth, leaving the pup struggling to breathe with it's head still enclosed in the membrane.

If this happens, tear the membrane away from the head with your fingers and wipe the nose and mouth, then, if the pup is still attached to the bitch by the cord, (the afterbirth still not having come away from the bitch) use the Artery Clamp, clamping it onto the cord about 2.5cm (2ins) away from the pup, being careful not to pull the cord where it is attached to the naval.

Also be very careful not to pinch the skin of the bitch's vulva with the clamp.

The reason for using the clamp is to stop the afterbirth slipping back into the bitch when you free the puppy.

Next break the cord using either, finger nails (clean), or a blunt pair of scissors. A ragged tear is more natural and bleeds less, if at all. If the bleeding does not stop almost immediately, tie the end of the cord with a piece of cotton soaked in iodine, but do not do this if it is not really necessary.

If the pup and the afterbirth both come away together, leave breaking the cord for a minute or two to allow the blood in the placenta to drain into the pup. Making sure the pup is breathing properly is more important than detaching it in this case.

If the pup is being a bit slow to get going and the bitch is being very possessive about it you can distract her by cutting the cord and giving her the afterbirth to eat. This is natural for her and is a valuable food source.

Let her have the pup back as soon as you are sure it is all right. If it's breathing seems a bit 'snuffly', as may well be the case if it has been born hind feet first and inhaled some fluid, hold it head down, but well supported and swing it gently from side to side to drain it.

Then let the bitch finish stimulating it, which she will do by licking it and pushing it about. It looks rough but doesn't seem to do them any harm.

The second pup may arrive fairly soon after the first, then there may be a longer wait between the second and third, or third and fourth. This is presuming a litter of three, four or five pups. This pause is usually due to the fact that during a normal whelping, one horn of the uterus empties first and the pause seems to cover the change over to the other horn starting to contract.

This pause can be used to make sure that the pups have had their first feed. Their suckling will stimulate the next lot of contractions.

This feed is most important as the first milk contains Colostrum which carries the antibodies which will give the pups protection against disease for the first few weeks of their lives. They are much less likely to get sick at the early stage than when they reach seven or eight weeks old when this immunity from the dam begins to wear off. The puppy's gut is only permeable by the Colostrum for a few hours so it is very important to make sure that each one of them has had a good feed as soon as possible.

They may be lying close up against the bitch and look as if they are feeding, but do check that they are latched on and sucking.

If the bitch seems to be having a bit of a rest after producing a couple of pups, offer her a drink of warm milk with a teaspoon of glucose and a crushed calcium tablet in it.

Don't forget that she may well want to relieve herself after the whelping, especially if she has had a couple of drinks during this time. If she doesn't settle after the last pup has been born, this may well be all that is wrong with her.

You will have to take her outside as she will be very reluctant to leave the pups. TAKE A TORCH with you if it is dark, there may be another pup yet to come and it won't be the first to be born on the lawn.

Never see the first couple of pups into the world and then go to bed leaving the bitch to 'get on with it'. You may come down in the morning to 'stillborn' pups which need not have been with a little timely assistance from you... or even a dead bitch. There are many things which can go wrong even after two normal deliveries.

You have planned the mating, paid the stud fee and waited for nine weeks for this event: one night's lost sleep is not a lot to sacrifice and you owe it to your bitch to care for her properly.

After the last pup has been born, presuming all has gone normally, the bitch should settle down to washing and feeding her litter. If she still seems restless there may be one more pup to come, probably from higher up in the horn. I have had a puppy born eight hours after the other four. Unfortunately it was dead. This pup could probably have been saved by a caesarean section, but I was whelping the bitch for someone else and they would rather have lost the pup than subject their adored bitch to an operation.

In this case, it was probably wise because it was very difficult to get this bitch to settle to her maternal duties anyway; if she had been confused by coming round from the anaesthetic, she may not have recognised them as her children.

If your bitch does have to have a caesarean, especially if she is a maiden, do make sure she has accepted the pups before you consider leaving her alone with them. A friend of mine came down in the morning to a whelping box covered with blood and mangled bodies, where the bitch in her confused state had killed all four pups after a caesarean delivery.

Getting back to your whelping. If you have seen the afterbirth from each pup as it was born, all well and good, but sometimes they do not come away with the pup and slip back inside the uterus.

If this does happen, bear it in mind whilst watching your bitch carefully for the next few days. Usually they break down and come away over the next few days as a brownish discharge, but they can cause infection with a consequent rise in temperature.

It is very important to take your bitch's temperature every day after the whelping until it returns to normal. It is usual for it to rise to around 102 degrees for a day or so. If it goes above this then some infection has set in and you will need to get a course of penicillin from your vet.

There are various types of penicillin, make sure that you get the one that is safe to give to a nursing bitch. Any other kind may cause you to have 'fading puppies'.

Be very careful about giving any medicine to a pregnant or nursing bitch and always check with your vet first. If she should have to visit the vet with any illness during her pregnancy, remember to tell him that she is pregnant when he is prescribing medicine. Cortisone can cause abortions.

There is an increased risk of infection for a bitch and puppies in a kennel where a lot of litters are born. If you do get 'fading puppies' this could be due to a virus harboured by unhygenic conditions.

'Fading puppies' are those which just seem to give up. They stop feeding and resist all efforts to keep them alive. It is impossible to be germ free, but one can ensure minimum risk by disinfecting whelping boxes and boiling scissors etc. before use.

After all the pups are born, check them for any deformities such a hind dew claws or cleft palates, the last could be the cause if the pup seems unable to suckle. If you have a breed where it is accepted practice to remove all dew claws this should be done by the vet when the pups are two to three days old. If hind dew claws are missed until after this stage it will mean an operation under anaesthetic later in life to take them off.

Do put Vet Bed in the whelping box. The pups can move well on it, reaching their dam easily. There is nothing worse than watching the poor little things struggling and sliding about on slippery newspaper. 'Vet Bed' will keep them warm and dry as the moisture goes straight through it.

PUPPY REARING

For three weeks you should need to do very little for the pups beyond ensuring that they are kept warm, draught free and quiet. Use a heated pad underneath part of the Vet Bed, and keep the box covered to darken it. I am not much in favour of heat lamps, they tend to draw the cold air up so that the pups are in a permanent draught, consequently it is difficult to get the temperature correct.

If you do have to use a heat lamp, make sure that there is room in the whelping box for the pups and bitch to escape from the heat if necessary.

If the puppies are lying spaced out all round the box, they are too hot. If piled on top of one another, they are too cold. A greenhouse thermometer placed on the Vet Bed under the lamp will tell you if you are cooking them or not.

Correct temperature for them at the beginning of their lives should be around 87F. The following table is a guide to whelping box temperatures when rearing orphan pups, or when the bitch is not present:-

1st week	. . . .	91-86F
2nd week	. . . .	86-82F
3rd week	. . . .	82-79F
4th week	. . . .	79-75F

The bitch's mammary glands give off a lot of heat at this time and, unless it is freezing mid-winter, as long as she is with them, gentle heat from underneath is all the puppies need.

Their eyes will open naturally around twelve to fourteen days, do not try to assist this procedure. The retina is not developed at birth, but at four weeks their vision is as good as an adults. They are also deaf at first, but are hearing at about two weeks and hearing as well as an adult at about four weeks.

Under normal circumstances the puppies should double their birthweight by about 10 days old.

If a puppy cries a lot during the first few days of life, especially if the bitch rejects it and pushes it away to a corner of the box, you are probably going to lose it. At this age there is very little the vet can do. The bitches instinct is nearly always right and I have learned to trust it.

I have lost four pups like this. One took too long before the vet and I managed to get it to breathe at birth, and suffered brain damage. This one was destroyed at two days old as it was crying miserably and seemed unable to suckle.

The second one, as I previously mentioned had peritonitis.

The third, which was crying and not feeding, I had put down, and on post mortem it was found to have a completely solid section of intestine, the rest of the intestine was deformed as well.

The fourth, which died at four days was found to have improperly inflated lungs.

Until a pup is born, the blood supply from the dam by-passes the lungs which are deflated. At the moment of birth, nature miraculously re-routes the blood supply through the lungs to allow them to inflate, and breathing to start. During whelping it is vitally important to make sure the pup is breathing properly before handing it back to the bitch.

All these puppies which had to be put down were dispatched by my vet with an injection. I have heard some fairly horrific stories from other breeders who talk of drowning pups, or 'knocking them on the head'. This sickens me. Please have the job done painlessly by your vet.

About two weeks after the pups are born you may find that your bitch would like to be away from them at times. Please ensure that she can escape when she wishes.

At about three weeks, carefully cut the sharp tips off the pups claws or they will scratch the bitch while they are feeding. A pair of ordinary nail clippers are best for this job. Take great care not to cut too much off because you will cut through the vein which runs down the nail, causing it to bleed. This also hurts the puppies.

WEANING

When your puppies are four weeks old you can start offering them solid food in the shape of some minced beef once a day, about a teaspoonful for a small breed.

At the same time always keep a small dish of fresh water in the whelping box, you will find that they will drink from it. The dish needs to be heavy glass or earthenware to avoid being tipped up.

By the beginning of the fifth week they should be eating the meat well and you will have to increase the amount... I always feed to appetite.

This is the time when the bitch would naturally begin to wean them by regurgitating her food for them. I have had one who carried lumps of her own dinner into the box to offer them.

Having eaten her food, the bitch will probably go into the whelping box and stand while the pups suckle... after about a minute this will stimulate her to regurgitate her dinner into a corner of the box for them to eat, this is perfectly natural, your bitch is not ill or being sick.

At the age of five weeks, ease the puppies onto the same food that their dam eats. I do not agree with those who advise feeding dogs on Farex and other baby foods. These are designed for humans and are unsuitable for dogs.

Puppies never seem to have upset tummies at weaning when fed on the same food as their dams regular diet. After all this was what they were getting through the blood supply when they were in the womb, and subsequently through the milk supply, so their bodies are ready adjusted to processing it.

Do not try to forcibly wean your puppies; as long as their dam will feed them, let her. They are still receiving antibodies through her milk supply.

Let her stay with them until they leave for their new homes and they will end up better behaved, having received a few sharp corrections from her for excessive biting or just generally being a nuisance.

A lot of temperament problems can be cured between five and eight weeks old when the puppies are very receptive to gentle but firm correction for excessive noise or bullying their brothers and sisters.

Weather permitting, the puppies should now be spending some time outside in the fresh air.

Always make sure they have water and shade in their runs and don't forget that the sun moves round very quickly, and that a puppy up to the age of seven or eight weeks is not yet able to control its body temperature very efficiently.

Their bed should be in the shade as they will only play for about twenty minutes before needing some sleep.

WORMING

Worm the puppies when they are four weeks old unless any of them have upset stomachs and loose motions. If this is the case, leave the worming until they are all better.

For very small breeds, half of a Citrazine tablet will be enough. I have been told to give them a tablet, but in my experience this much can quite frequently make them ill and be sick before the tablet has taken effect.

When you have dosed the puppies, keep the bitch away from them for four hours or so, or she may clear up after them and ingest a hefty dose of worms and Citrazine herself. Leave worming the bitch until a week after you have done the puppies.

Dose the pups again at around seven weeks, using the same dose. You may not see any worms after this dose, probably the four week old worms were too immature to have laid eggs.

Bitches naturally clear up after their very young puppies and I have had several bitches feel unwell at around the four week period of rearing puppies, culminating in two or three days of sickness and diarrhoea. This is best treated by not allowing her to clear up, and by starving her for a day. Just allow her sips of boiled water with natural organic honey in it.

When she feels well enough to eat again, offer her lightly scrambled egg, and if that stays down and she seems hungry, follow it up with boiled white fish and boiled white rice. Never try to force her to eat, starving is positively beneficial in these cases and she knows best what her body needs. Do NOT give her milk, it is not a natural food for an adult dog and it curdles in the stomach. She should, if possible, have access to some couch grass to help with internal cleansing.

Ease her back on to her normal diet gradually, and always include some garlic in her feed, two or three times a week. It is a marvellous internal antiseptic and natural wormer. It also goes through the bitches milk and helps to worm the puppies.

Garlic will deter fleas too, as it seeps through to the skin, and it is beneficial in cases of respiratory infection such as Kennel Cough.

SELLING PUPPIES
At eight weeks old, your puppies should be ready to go to their new homes. As a responsible breeder you should have a few questions to ask of your prospective purchasers to ensure that your pups will have a long and happy life.

Genuine dog lovers don't mind being given the 'third degree' as they know it is for the dogs benefit.

Questions should be something on the following lines:-

1) Is there someone at home all day.

2) Do they have a safely fenced garden.

3) Do ALL members of the family want a dog.

4) Are there any children under ten years old in the family.
   If the puppy is to be a present for the child, I like to meet that child and see it with the puppy. Puppies are not toys, and unless the situation is handled very carefully, the puppy will probably attach itself to the lady of the house, which could upset the child and cause problems.

5) Are there any other dogs in the household, and if there are, what sex and breed. If the resident dog is very protective of its owners it may well resent a newcomer, even going to the lengths of killing it.

   Never forget that the dog retains all its wild instincts underneath a thin veneer of our imposed civilization.

FINALLY... Please do not sell puppies just before Christmas, if people want them for Christmas presents, having ensured that it is a good home, keep the puppy until after the festivities have died down. It is hard enough on a puppy having to adjust to a new home without being pitched into a madhouse of people having parties and making a lot of noise, and with no-one having the time to settle the pup in gently.

People usually don't mind if you explain this to them, and if they do, they are probably not the right kind of prospective owner anyway.

Give your puppies a thorough examination when they are seven weeks old. Check them for dandruff, which can be removed by shampooing with the baby preparation Crado-Cap, obtainable from the chemist. Look into the ears and if they are dirty, treat them with G.A.C. drops which you can get from your vet. Do not put powder in their ears, it can set like concrete.

Look for signs of fleas, there are powder and shampoos which can be used on small puppies, but do check the labels on the bottles to confirm that they are suitable.

NEVER spray your dogs with an anti-flea preparation in an enclosed area, or confine them in a kennel after spraying. These sprays contain a nerve gas. Three retrievers, which were sprayed and then shut away together in their kennel, died from the gas.

Get all the paperwork done in advance... it is impossible to talk to the new owners when they come for the puppy, whilst writing out pedigrees and diet sheets.

The diet sheet should state exactly what you have fed the puppy and the times that it was fed. You can also help the puppy to settle into its new home by giving its normal rest times, and roughly when it has been used to going out to relieve itself.

Suggest to the new owners that they clean the pups teeth fairly regularly... it has obviously never occurred to most of them that one can. There are special doggy toothpastes on the market. An ordinary toothbrush with the bristles cut down is quite suitable.

They should also not let the toenails grow too long if the dog is not getting enough roadwork to keep them short.

Remind them that their puppy is still a baby and will need a lot of sleep; in a quiet warm place that it knows as it's own. Preferably not a basket, they are draughty and are liable to be chewed producing splinters, or one of those pretty foam creations. I have known them to disintegrate all over the kitchen overnight. A cardboard box is best, with an old blanket or some vet bed until the puppy has finished teething.

If the puppy has started its course of injections, the Vets Certificate should be given to the new owner.

Give a receipt for the purchase price and write any special arrangements on it. If the puppy is Kennel Club Registered, give the registration certificate.

Send the puppy off with enough of its regular food to cover the first few days, and a piece of blanket which it has been sleeping on with its brothers and sisters to see it through the first few lonely nights. Suggest to the new owners that they give it a hot water bottle, placed under the Vet Bed, to cuddle up to.

Finally, all responsible breeders should offer to take back, or help to re-home a puppy if the purchaser can no longer keep it for any reason.

If your buyer is no longer in the first flush of youth try, tactfully, to get them to put in writing somewhere that, should anything happen to them, the dog will come back to you for re-homing. This will probably ensure that you are doubly careful where you place your pups so that they have good loving homes, and don't come bouncing back to you.

I have only had four returned to me in 10 years, and all for perfectly acceptable reasons. It is a good idea to refund the purchase price, you may lose a little on the resale, but you will build up a lot of goodwill and hopefully know where the pups you have bred are at all times.

"DON'T PANIC" BY WENDY LEWIS
(ALSO AVAILABLE IN BOOKLET DIRECT FROM WENDY LEWIS)

The Original Breed Standard (NO LONGER USED)

THE LANCASHIRE HEELER CLUB

President: Mrs G. Mackintosh

Chairman:	*Secretary:*	*Treasurer:*
Mr P. Welch	Mrs G. Lowe	Miss H. Church

OFFICIAL STANDARD OF THE LANCASHIRE HEELER
AS APPROVED AT THE CLUB MEETING HELD ON JULY 1st, 1978

General Description: This is a low-set, small, yet strong and active worker. Always happy when working cattle in a manner expected of a heeler, yet with his strong terrier characteristics apparent when hunting rabbits or exterminating rats. Common with most working breeds the Lancashire Heeler displays true affection to all members of the household and is always ready to protect the home or the car whenever these are left to his care. It is a breed which must appeal to those demanding all these qualities in such a small breed with a coat which requires the minimum of daily attention and which never leaves white hairs around.

The Head: This must be proportionate to the rest of the dog, the skull flat and wide between the ears, it tapers gradually towards the eyes which are set wide apart, should be dark, almond shaped, not too small nor too large. The stop at this point should be equal in distance from the nose and the occiput, the tapering to continue along the foreface top to be parallel, showing neither downface nor dishface. Lips to be firm, teeth white and level with the upper incisors fitting closely in front of the lower incisors. Undershot or obviously overshot mouths not to be encouraged, often puppies with overshot mouths grow into adults with correct mouths. The stop to be obvious but not too exaggerated. Ears to show an alert lift or erect, but houndlike ears not to be encouraged.

The Neck: To be of moderate length, let into shoulders which lay well back.

Elbows: To be firm against the ribs, legs with ample bone and showing a slight turn at the pastern, allowing the feet to turn slightly outwards, this must not be exaggerated to the point of being weak at pastern and to destroy freedom of movement.

The Feet: To be smallish, firm and with well padded cushions.

The Body: This must have well sprung ribs which extend well back, leaving a close coupling. The topline always firm and perfectly level, never showing a dip at withers nor a fall-away at the croup. Height taken at shoulder should be about

12 inches for males and 10 inches for females, the body length taken from the shoulder point to the set-on of tail to be approximately one inch more than shoulder height. A variation from these figures permissible, but considerable deviation should not be encouraged.

The Tail: This should be set-on high must not be docked, but carried over the back when dog has been alerted and may curve, but not form a tight ring as seen in Pugs.

The Hindquarters: These must be muscular with hocks let down and when viewed from the rear they should when standing and moving remain parallel, never being bandy or cow-hocked.

The Coat: This may vary according to the seasons from a shiny sleek short coat, to a longer coat showing longer hair at mane, but not to be too long or stand-offish as in Chows.

The Colour: This is to be black with deep mahogany tan markings on the muzzle, spots on the cheeks and often over the eyes, from the knees downwards with a desirable thumb-mark immediately above the feet, inside the hindlegs and under the tail, description of the marking should not be too detailed, most important is they provide the desired appearance. The richness of the tan deteriorates with age and allowance should be made when judging older dogs. The preferred colour should not include any white whatsoever. A small white spot on forechest is permissible and ought not to debar an otherwise good specimen from being placed, at the same time it should not be encouraged. White in any other place to be penalised so as not to encourage the spread of white markings.

NOTES

NOTES

NOTES